T0162115

DEATH IN CALIFORNIA

The Bizarre, Freakish and Just Curious
Ways People Die in the Golden State

DAVID KULCZYK

B O O K S

Linden Publishing
Fresno, CA

Published by Craven Street Books,
an imprint of Linden Publishing.
2006 S. Mary, Fresno, California, 93721
559-233-6633 / 800-345-4447
CravenStreetBooks.com

Craven Street Books is a trademark of Linden Publishing, Inc.

Craven Street Books project cadre:
James Goold, Carla Green, Doris Hall, John David Marion, Stephen
Blake Mettee, Kent Sorsky

ISBN: 978-1-884995-57-6
135798642

Printed in the USA on acid-free paper.

Library of Congress Cataloging-in-Publication Data

Kulczyk, David.
  Death in California : the bizarre, freakish, and just curious ways people
die in the Golden State / by David Kulczyk.
     p. cm.
  Includes bibliographical references and index.
  ISBN 978-1-884995-57-6 (pbk. : alk. paper)
  1. California--History--Anecdotes. 2. California--Biography--
Anecdotes. 3. Death--California--History--Anecdotes. 4. Accidents--
California--History--Anecdotes. 5. Violent deaths--California--
History--Anecdotes. 6. Murder--California--History--Anecdotes.
I. Title.

  F861.6.K85 2009
  303.609794--dc22

                                    20090214805

Versions of *The Wheatland Hop Riot* and *Death House* appeared in the
Sacramento News and Review on August 30, 2007, and February 21,
2008, respectively.

DEATH IN CALIFORNIA

This book is dedicated to Carl Kulczyk
(April 5, 1952 – June 3, 2008)

Contents

Acknowledgments

I would like to thank my wife Donna for giving me the time and space to do this project. I'd also like to thank Eric Schumacher-Rasmussen for editing most of the manuscript and Ryan Schumacher (no relation to Eric) for picking up the ball and helping with the editing when Eric had emergencies. I'd also like to thank Carson Hendricks at the Sacramento Archives and Museum Collection Center, the Los Angeles Public Library, everyone at the California State Library and NewspaperArchive.com. Great thanks also go to Lorraine Clarke, Brian Balentine, Earl Brooks, Steve Mettee, Megan Reilly, Kent Sorsky, James Kulczyk, Richard Sinn, James Van Ochten, Martin Imbach, John Massoni, Wendy Oshima, Cynthia Shepard, Susan Kendzulak and Luke Suminski.

Introduction

Death in California, said the headlines in the newspapers back east. Locals eagerly scanned the list for friends and relatives who'd headed out to California to strike it rich in the far-off canyons of the Sierra Nevada Mountains. Fast-forward to over 150 years later and "Death in California" is still an almost-daily headline in the world's newspapers. California has always been a destination for people with dreams of fame and fortune, whether it be found in the gold mines, on the silver screen, or in the lush green fields. Anything is possible in California, and when anything is possible, Death always lurks nearby. And Death doesn't care one bit about your dreams, nor your social status, religion, or race.

The vastness of California is almost unfathomable. Its 163,696 square miles are filled with mountains, waterfalls, deserts, lakes, streams, cliffs, canyons, and sheer rock ledges. At 14,505 feet, Mount Whitney is the tallest mountain in the Lower Forty-Eight, and it's just one of the fourteen mountains in California that soar above 14,000 feet in the state's more than 100 separate mountain ranges. Forty-five percent of the surface area in California is covered by forest; at the other end of the geographic and climatological spectrum, the state boasts more than 25,000 square miles of desert.

California has three of the most highly populated cities in the United States, with Los Angeles at number two (3.8 million), San Diego number eight (1.4 million), and San Jose coming in at number ten (almost 1 million in the city proper and 1.8 million in the metro area). Five other cities rank in the top fifty. If California were a separate country, it would be in the top forty in population and the tenth-biggest economy in the world.

Before the invasion of the Europeans, most of the seventy different groups of native Californians barely knew what murder was. They lived in a virtual paradise with plenty of game, fish, and vegetation to eat. Over the centuries the different tribes had adjusted to the climate they lived in and they lived as one with nature. Coastal natives became great fishermen, while the valley natives used the rich soil and plentiful water to grow crops. They traded with and married into neighboring tribes and got along peacefully. If a situation became violent, they still did their best not to kill each other. If a brave did kill a member of another tribe during warfare, the killer's family had to make amends with the family of the victim with gifts of hides, meat, and goods. It was outlandish for natives to commit murder, as they would be banished by their families from their village and snubbed by neighboring villages and tribes. They would become outcasts in a society that was built on family and tribal cooperation.

Human society in California existed in this way for centuries. Then, in 1519, Spain invaded the Western Hemisphere and started a 300-year reign of terror against all aboriginal tribes residing there. For 200 years, the Spanish had no interest in the vast coast north of Mexico. Their interest was mainly in the gold and silver that was mined by captive natives in Mexico and Peru. When word hit Spain that England and Russia had sent exploratory fleets to examine the immense western coast of North America, they quickly sent troops and the ever-present Catholic missionaries to set up missions and establish a visible presence to dissuade any other nations from the thought of planting their flags in California.

In 1769, the Spanish established the Presidio of San Diego and quickly started a system of Jesuit missions up the coast, each a one-day mule ride from any other. Eventually, a chain of missions led from San Diego to Sonoma, north of San Francisco. The idea was to have a Spanish presence in California and to spread the Catholic faith to the native people they considered to be godless savages. But along with Christianity, the Spanish brought European diseases to which the California natives were susceptible, and in a matter of a few years, 80 percent of the aboriginal population was dead.

When gold was discovered at Sutter's Mill in 1848, things went from bad to worse for the native tribes. Their land and way of life were trampled by technologically advanced invaders and, by 1850, their entire world was in turmoil. The atrocities carried out on the Plains Indians pale when compared to the outright genocide that happened to the Native Americans in California. A hundred Pomo Indians were massacred at Clearlake in 1850, followed by massacres in 1852, 1853, and 1855 by federal troops and local vigilantes in Northern California. Bounties were paid for heads and scalps of the members of the northern tribes. Young boys popped Indians for sport. The native women were raped and turned into prostitutes by unscrupulous men. The native children were adopted or sold into slavery.

After extensive negotiations between the Shasta tribes and Siskiyou County miners, ranchers, and businessmen, an accord was signed on November 4, 1851. Thousands of Shastas were in attendance for the treaty signing, which was followed by a feast of beef and bread. Unfortunately for the Shastas, the bread was poisoned and it is estimated that 6,000 Indians either died from the poison or were killed later when they were hunted down by gun-toting, hate-filled maniacs.

The Indian Census of 1852 reported only twenty-seven Native Americans living in Siskiyou County. The natives were over-whelmed, and within two decades were essentially decimated.

Few of the 49ers suffered more than the natives, but it was still extremely dangerous for the gold seekers. The tor-turous trip overland killed thousands of emigrants through accidents and disease. The six-month sea journey was just as treacherous as the land route. Hundreds died on the Isth-mus of Panama, catching a jungle fever while waiting for a ship to San Francisco. The leaking ships were overcrowded, underventilated, and ill-supplied. Many of the ships weren't shipshape enough for the voyage and never even made it to the Golden Gate.

Once the emigrants arrived, they faced avalanches and cave-ins, dysentery and starvation, hypothermia, drowning, and boiler explosions on riverboats. The abundant California grizzly bear had no fear of humans and could effortlessly de-capitate a man with one swipe of its giant paw. Seemingly dis-tant thunderstorms could flood a peaceful canyon in seconds, carrying off campsites and depositing bodies miles away.

On top of the natural disasters, the criminal element of society were some of the first arrivals in the Golden State. Countless emigrants were mugged, bushwhacked, and mur-dered for a watch or a few pieces of gold. Few people carried any kind of identification, and bodies simply were buried where they had died.

There are obvious dangers to living in a large city, but few think about the danger that lurks in the rich farmland and scenic vineyards of California. Farming is a highly mechanized industry, and the long distances to an emer-gency room can quickly turn an injury into a fatality. There are hundreds of ways to get killed on a farm: chains break, rods get thrown, grain elevators explode, livestock stam-pede. Over the years, hundreds of Californians have been killed by horses and mules.

Anyone who has ever driven on the winding mountain roads and vanishing-point highways in California knows the temptation to drive fast. The car culture may have gotten its start in Detroit, but it revved into high gear in California. What most people forget about the good old days before safety glass, seat belts, and air bags is that a minor fender-bender could produce fatalities. You only have to read any local newspaper from that era to realize that seat belts really do save lives.

From tourists being swept to their death over Vernal Fall in pastoral Yosemite National Park to blues/boogie singer Bob Bear Hite overdosing on heroin in a seedy Hollywood nightclub; from the anonymous Mexican teenager murdered by Gordon Northcott on an isolated chicken ranch to President Warren G. Harding dying mysteriously in office while in San Francisco, death in California never stops to see who you are.

For many inmates of Folsom Prison, the graveyard was the only way out. *Sacramento Archives and Museum Collection Center (SAMCC)*

Until the introduction of safety belts, simple accidents lead to fatalities.
Sacramento Archives and Museum Collection Center (SAMCC)

CHAPTER 1

The Bowman Incident

Monroeville, Colusa County
March 9, 1852

We all like to think of the founders of the great state of California as strong, independent, and upright citizens, soberly blazing a path through the dangerous wilderness, fighting primitive natives, and fending off attacks from grizzly bears and mountain lions so that future settlers could reside in relative peace and prosperity. While the explorers were certainly strong and independent, they were basically mountain men, uncouth and uneducated. While in the backwoods they lived more like the Native Americans than contemporary Americans, except unlike the aboriginals of North America, the mountain men never bathed. Once among their own kind, their gatherings resembled an outlaw motorcyclist convention with horses more than the pastoral paintings that we've all seen in banks and government buildings. This was never truer than the circumstances surrounding the murder of Levi Sigler on March 9, 1852, in what is now Tehama County.

William C. Moon, Ezekiel Merritt, and Peter Lassen were some of the first Caucasians to settle in Northern California. In 1845, the three men went in together on a business venture selling grindstones that they quarried from Stony Creek, just south of Hamilton City in Glenn County. While Lassen went on to blaze his ill-fated Lassen Cutoff Trail and to be mysteriously murdered on April 26, 1859, Moon and Merritt continued to be involved in various business ventures together.

Merritt was described as a coarse-grained, loud-mouthed, unprincipled, whiskey-drinking, quarrelsome fellow with a speech impediment. He was also called Stuttering Merritt, but probably not to his face.

Moon, affectionately called Old Moon by his contemporaries, first entered California in 1841 with the Workman Party. He explored the Golden State with General John Bidwell during the 1844 expedition and unsuccessfully petitioned for a land grant from the Mexican government. During the winter of 1845–1846, Moon built an adobe house on the Sacramento River in Tehama County, southeast of Red Bluff. His combination inn, tavern, and supply shop was an active staging ground for the 1846 Bear Flag Revolution, after which the Mexican government relinquished California to the United States. Moon's adobe has been called the Cradle of California Liberty and the Birthplace of the Bear Flag Revolt.

When Moon wasn't supplying alcohol and food to the revolutionaries, he ran a ferry across the Sacramento River. Moon had no problem enslaving his native neighbors to row his ferry for him because, for them, that was better than working in his mines. His business prospered by the sweat of native labor, and by 1850 he was able to build a new building, known as the Moon Rancho.

The Moon Rancho was a two-story, oak-timber building with a brick foundation about one hundred yards from the Moon adobe. The ground floor had two rooms, one a store and bar and the other a combination kitchen/dining room. Four sleeping rooms were upstairs. The business must have been a welcoming sight to the travelers entering the Sacramento Valley.

Around the same time Moon built the rancho, the first session of the California legislature met and divided the state into twenty-seven counties. The Moon Rancho was located in the giant county of Colusi, which at that time consisted of what are now portions of Glenn, Tehama, Shasta, Butte and Colusa counties. The county seat of Colusi County was Monroeville, which no longer exists. The village rested on the west side of the Sacramento River, a couple of miles below the confluence of Stony Creek and the mighty Sacramento River. Named after Uriah P. Monroe, Colusa County's first county clerk, the site was picked out of convenience; the proximity to the river made it easy to access.

The county clerk owned the largest building in the county. The two-story Monroe House was the main structure in Monroeville and was built from the wreckage of the steamboat *California*, which in 1850 hit a snag and sank near the town. The Monroe House served as the courthouse as well as saloon, store, hotel, and post office. Monroe charged fifty dollars a month in rent for the courtroom facilities.

Meanwhile, back at the Moon Rancho, Oregonian Nathaniel Bowman came knocking on March 9, 1852. Bowman, who called himself a stock trader and miner, was passing through the area on his way back to his home in Oregon, where he had lived since 1847. He had visited his brother in Napa and stopped by the Moon adobe to deliver a letter from his brother to Old Moon. Moon and the Bowmans were cousins. He found Moon at the adobe along with Moon's Indian wife Sal, John McCord, Louis Bercier, and Bowman's old friend Levi Sigler and his Indian spouse, whose name was not recorded.

Bowman and Sigler greeted each other with a bear hug. They were both old mountain men who had come out West before any other Caucasians. They were now witnessing the end of the pristine wilderness and the onslaught of one of the greatest migrations of humans in the history of the world.

They were both in the autumn of their lives and looking for a better and less physical way of making a living. Sigler worked around the rancho for Moon, and Bowman occasionally did the same.

The group settled in for the night, which in California in the mid-1850s meant getting completely drunk. Bowman, along with McCord and Bercier, stumbled over to Moon's tavern, about a hundred yards from the adobe, to get more brandy. McCord and Bercier worked for a stage company that was based at the Moon Rancho, and by all accounts they were decent men.

According to statements by McCord and Bercier, Bowman was so drunk that he fell off the box that he was sitting on and would have fallen into a roaring fire had not one of the patrons caught him. He fell down several more times, and was too drunk to join in a card game.

Arriving back at the adobe about ten, the men put an equally falling-down-drunk Sigler on his blanket next to his Indian wife. Everyone prepared for bed. Bowman got into bed with Moon and his wife, with Moon in the middle. McCord and Bercier got into the other bed together. A bed was a luxury not to be wasted by one person in those days.

After about twenty minutes, Bowman got out of bed. Thinking that Sigler was passed out cold, he started putting the moves on Sigler's Native American companion. But Sigler was awake and sternly told Bowman what he thought about his old friend trying to do such a thing. Then came the sound of the breaking of glass and the splintering of wood.

Bercier lit a candle just in time to see Bowman beating Sigler with a broken chair. Everyone in the cabin yelled at Bowman to stop.

"Let me finish him first," was Bowman's reply as he struck Sigler two more times.

Sigler was very dead.

McCord jumped out of bed and swore at Bowman. He wanted to know why Bowman would do such a thing. Bowman responded by slashing McCord across the forehead with a knife. McCord ran to the tavern to get a pistol, but it wasn't necessary, as Bowman followed and turned himself in. He was placed in bartender Nathaniel Merrill's room. Again, beds being such a luxury in old California, Merrill slept next to the murderer that night, although he claimed that he wasn't very comfortable.

The next morning at breakfast, Bowman didn't understand what the fuss was all about. He announced that he did not consider that he had killed anything more than a damn coyote. Bowman's time was over. It was no longer acceptable for a flea-bitten, buckskin-clad, drunken mountain man to murder a longtime friend. California was now a state and although most of it was a remote wilderness, there were now laws on the books concerning the prosecution of murder.

Five armed men took Bowman eighteen miles south to Monroeville and turned him over to Sheriff J. F. Willis. He was placed under guard in an adobe building owned by Uriah P. Monroe.

The population of Colusi County at the time was 620 people, and only 400 were Caucasian males. Foreigners, females, Native Americans and Negroes weren't allowed to vote. Due to the lack of interest and viable candidates, William B. Ide was reluctantly Colusi County's justice of the peace, county judge, deputy county clerk, deputy clerk of the district court, deputy county auditor, county treasurer, deputy county surveyor, and coroner.

As coroner, the former commandant of the Bear Flag Revolt was responsible for the inquiry into the murder. Nathaniel Merrill, the Moon Rancho bartender and bedmate of Bowman, was the foreman of the coroner's jury. Arriving at the scene, they found Sigler's bloody body straightened out and covered with a cloth. His head was beaten so badly that he was barely recognizable. He had defensive wounds on his hands and a knife wound through his cheek. A trail of dried blood mapped out the murder, and it appeared that Sigler was trying to escape while enduring the attack.

Nathaniel Bowman pleaded not guilty to the murder of Levi Sigler at the Monroe House. Unusual for the times, a preliminary hearing and a grand jury was called to go over the evidence of the murder. Sigler's name was tarnished by a series of witness testimonies that accused him of being a very bad and dangerous man. A month earlier, Moon and Merrill had chased Sigler off the ranch because of his threatening behavior, but he was allowed back to the Moon Rancho soon afterwards.

Bowman went on the stand and said that he indeed tried to seduce Sigler's Indian companion, but she recoiled at the request and woke up her husband. Fearing that Sigler would kill him, he decided to hurt him enough so that Sigler would not be able to harm him. Bowman didn't explain the knife wounds.

On March 12, 1852, the grand jury returned with the indictment of Bowman and filed a written petition recommending that the county hire four suitable men to guard the prisoner and, if he were found guilty, to carry out the execution. William Ide, now acting as the county judge and presiding judge of the court of session, rejected the petition for guards. Bowman escaped that evening.

Bowman's only option was to head south into the Sacramento Valley. Everyone to the north and west would recognize him, and the Sacramento River was too high and swift with the spring runoff to cross to the east. Ten miles south of Monroeville, Bowman pounded on the cabin door of William H. Shephard, waking him from a deep sleep. Shephard recognized Bowman immediately, as he had been a member of the grand jury panel that had investigated the Sigler murder earlier that day. Even if he hadn't been present at the hearing, the chains that dangled from Bowman's limbs would have given him away as an escaped prisoner. Bowman politely asked Shephard if he would remove his chains. Shephard refused and told him that he was taking him back to Monroeville.

Bowman slipped away while Shephard was getting dressed, but was immediately caught after a short search. Shephard took Bowman to his neighbor's house, and together in the morning they returned Bowman to jail. The trial commenced on March 23 in Monroeville and had all the characteristics of the American court system. A respected judge, Winfield Scott Sherwood, presided over the case. Bowman had Dr. Robert Semple as his attorney. Semple was also a dentist and printer, but in 1849 he had been the president of the California Constitutional Convention. He was also the editor and cofounder of *The Californian*, the first newspaper published in California. The name of the prosecutor has been lost to history.

A jury of twelve men was assembled, and the trial began and ended later that day with a guilty verdict. Bowman didn't take the stand in his own defense, and female Native Americans were not allowed to testify as the laws of the State of California considered them incompetent as witnesses. The law declared that no Indian shall be permitted to give evidence in favor of, or against, any white person.

The next day the court came into order for the sentencing, which according to state law could only be death. Judge Sherwood set the execution date as April 24, 1852, at Monroeville. The prisoner was then taken to the Butte County jail to await execution.

Bowman was brought back to Monroeville on April 23rd for his last day on earth. He was kept under heavy guard in the adobe jail from which he had escaped a little over a month ago.

Nathaniel Bowman was cool and collected as he walked to the gallows. On the scaffold, Bowman addressed the assembled crowd that it had not been his intention to kill Sigler, but only to beat him badly. Sheriff Willis tripped the trapdoor and let Bowman hang for a half hour. It was his intention to kill Bowman, rather than let him ramble on and on about how he didn't mean to kill Sigler.

CHAPTER 2
A Decade of War

Butte County
1860 to 1870

By 1860, the Native Americans who had made California their home for tens of thousands of years had had enough of the foreign invaders who had overtaken their land, raped their women, and destroyed their culture. The natives had lived in tranquility for eons, trading and intermingling with each other with very few problems. California tribes rarely went to war, and when there were hostilities, they tried not to seriously hurt each other. If a male combatant killed a warring tribe member, the killer and his family would compensate the dead man's family with gifts. Food was plentiful and the weather beautiful, so there were very few reasons to fight. The California natives had so much spare time on their hands that they made puzzles and played sporting games.

That all changed with the discovery of gold at Sutter's Mill on January 24, 1848. Before then, the inland natives enjoyed a society relatively free from the influence of European culture. The Spanish and later the Mexicans kept their colonization close to the coastline to ensure a safe and quick escape if the Native Californians decided to organize and repel the invaders. The only inland outpost was Sutter's Fort in present-day Sacramento, an oasis of European culture in the middle of the wilderness. Except for fur trappers, the Europeans had little interest in the interior of California. But once gold was discovered and the flood of immigrants poured into the mountains and valleys, the way of life that the natives enjoyed was over.

Hordes of men came from all over the world, bringing their native tongues and cultures that were completely alien to the natives. The California Indians at first thought the invaders were homosexuals because they didn't bring any females with them. They also laughed at their lack of backwoods knowledge, but the naïve natives were quickly shocked into submission by the brutality and bloodlust of the invaders. Their women were raped, the children sold as slaves, and the men were either shot as if they were forest animals or put to work as manual laborers. The invaders destroyed their streams, forests, and grasslands with their haphazard mining techniques and carelessness. They slaughtered their fish and game and cut down their oak trees, on which the natives depended for acorns as their food staple. The invaders also brought diseases that obliterated the natives in genocidal numbers.

The Easterners saw the Native Californians as only a group of dirty savages and believed it was their God-given right to use and develop the paradise called California. Most of the immigrants were totally ignorant that there were hundreds of tribes and scores of different languages among them.

The remnants of the decimated tribes retreated higher into the Sierra Nevada Mountains, but the lure of gold kept the prospectors searching into ever-more-remote canyons and mountains, finally pushing the natives to the breaking point.

Ten miles north of Oroville, as the crow flies, was the settlement of Pentz. The town's name was a misspelling of the name of an early settler, M. Pence, an Ohioan with an initial for a first name and a mean streak for the natives who had lived in Butte County for six thousand years before Egypt's pyramids were built. In 1850, Pence took his earnings from mining gold and bought a four-hundred-acre ranch in the Messilla Valley, rolled up his sleeves, and planted a variety of fruit trees. Most of Butte County's Indian difficulties seemed to happen around Pentz, and Pence was the captain of the local militia, formed to protect the residents from the natives.

Defeated and dejected native Californians are reduced to homeless beggars.
California State Library

Pence's hostility toward the natives might have been rooted in an experience that occurred on his first New Year's Eve on his ranch. A group of six or seven natives came uninvited to his ranch and stayed all night. Pence was nervous about the natives, but there was little that he could do except let them stay. The band was reported to be Concows and their chief was among the visitors. When morning arrived, the natives were gone, along with all of Pence's cattle.

Pence gathered some friends together and caught up with the natives and the cattle. They wounded the chief, who swore revenge. But the chief was soon caught, brought back to Pentz, and lynched in front of the town's post office after a vote from whoever happened to be standing around at the time.

Throughout the 1850s, as the fish and game were exterminated by the invaders, the starving natives stole the settlers' cattle so they could eat. Out of revenge, they would ambush miners who had diverted their once fish-filled streams. But the invaders would always seek to settle the score, and then some.

Pence led settlers and miners on revenge raids on the natives, engaging in mass lynchings and massacres. It was essentially open season on the natives. The men were to be shot on sight, and the women were to be captured, raped, and pimped out as prostitutes. Captured native children were sold to farmers as laborers.

Somehow, with all the harvesting of fruit and killing of natives, Pence found the time in 1857 to marry Sophia Finn. They eventually had two sons, Watt and Layton, as the Indian troubles died down.

The miners destroyed rivers and entire ecosystems in their reckless search for gold. *California State Library*

However, in the spring of 1862, reports of Indian attacks on miners, loggers, and herdsmen in remote sections of Butte County started trickling in to Pentz, and M. Pence quickly helped raise another company of citizen soldiers for protection. They would soon need it.

On June 21, 1862, a band of Mill Creek Indians attacked the Hickok children, sixteen-year-old Ida, thirteen-year-old Minnie and an unnamed young boy, while they were picking blackberries near Rock Creek. Ida was shot, stripped naked, and violated by the natives. Minnie ran towards Rock Creek, but was shot and was later found face-down in the creek. Teamster Thomas Allen, who was guiding his wagon down from a sawmill surprised the natives, who shot him with seventeen arrows and left him dead on the road.

Pence's militia company quickly went in pursuit of the hostile natives and discovered the ghastly scene. They followed a grisly trail of the Hickok children's dead horses and shredded clothing stuck in the brush that covers the hills and decided that they would need to have a well-supplied posse to rescue the boy and take revenge on the natives. After delaying several days to stock up on supplies, the posse went in search for the young Hickok boy. Two weeks and thirty-seven miles later, the boy's mutilated body was found under a pile of rocks and brush. It appeared that he had been dragged by a rope around his neck, and his fingers, ears, and toes had been cut off. He was later buried next to his sisters in Chico.

While the rest of the United States was fighting to keep itself as a more perfect union during the war between the States, the settlers around Pentz were having a terrible time with native interactions. The notorious Mill Creek Indians, led by a cruel, six-toed native called Bigfoot, began vicious attacks in the early summer of 1863; the most despicable was the abduction and subsequent murder of the Lewis children on July 5 or 6 of that year.

Sam Lewis owned a ranch near Dry Creek off Cherokee Road. His children—eleven-year-old Jimmy, nine-year-old Arenia, and six-year-old Johnny—left their school together, along with their teacher and a couple of other students. They parted ways at Littlefield Creek. Little Johnny wasn't old enough to go to school, but Mrs. Lewis had allowed the little boy to go with his siblings that day.

Stopping for a drink of water, Jimmy was shot and fell face first into the water. Natives sprung out of the bushes and threw heavy rocks onto his lifeless body, while his sister and little brother trembled in fear.

A group of ten natives grabbed the surviving two children and headed for the hills, with Chief Bigfoot leading them. They forced the barefooted children to run through the rocky terrain, until they came to Nance Canyon, where they camped for the night. Arenia cuddled her little brother throughout the chilly night.

They left the camp early in the morning, and when Johnny started crying, four of the Mill Creek Indians took the little boy away and killed him. They rejoined the band, wearing his clothes.

After crossing several creeks, the band came across some of Captain Bidwell's cattle. They killed one and ate strips of meat raw. After making moccasins from the cowhide, the natives were ready to start hiking again, taking much of the beef along with them, but only after two of the natives expressed their desire to tear Arenia's two gold earrings out of her ear. The girl took the earrings out, causing the two natives to fight over who would get them. Arenia settled the matter by handing each of them an earring.

The native in charge of Arenia was crippled, and he was additionally encumbered by the stolen meat. He told the girl that he had been shot by a white man. The two lagged farther and farther behind the rest of the group and when they got to Big Chico Creek, Arenia asked if she could sit down. The lame native told her yes, but he told her he would shoot her if she moved off the boulder that she was sitting on. As soon as the natives were out of sight, Arenia rolled off the rock and scurried through the brush and down a creek. As she hid in the water, she could hear the natives looking for her. They eventually gave up and Arenia ran to the nearby Thomasson Ranch and safety.

After her ordeal, Arenia Lewis changed her name to Thankful. She lived to a ripe old age, marrying three times.

On August 26, 1865, a group of Mill Creek Indians raided the Workman Ranch, killing Miss Smith, who had just arrived from Australia, and an old man who went by the name English John. Miss Smith and English John were both mutilated and scalped, and their throats were slit. Mrs. Workman was gravely injured, but found the strength to crawl to a neighbor's home, where she told her story before she died.

The natives took everything of value from the Workman Ranch and walked down the road toward Cherokee. They fired on Joe Miller, the president of the First National

Bank of Chico, who was riding a mule. Miller escaped with a flesh wound and a newfound admiration for his fleet-footed mule.

A posse was formed that eventually numbered sixteen, and they went in search for the Mill Creek Indians with the intention of eliminating them once and for all. Deciding that the murderers would be at Black Rock on Mill Creek, the men found their trail, which took them past the deserted Hickok homestead. The men spent several days stalking the natives all the way back to their campsite, often crawling on their bellies as to not give away their position.

At daybreak on August 31, the men, led by the noted Indian-killer Hi Good, crawled near the Mill Creek Indians' campsite and opened fire on the sleeping natives, who had felt secure that they had gone so far into the wilderness that the ranchers would not follow.

The first native that Good shot was wearing Mr. Workman's stovepipe hat. After twenty minutes most of the Mill Creek Indians were dead. The few fleeing survivors took pot-shots at the white men and yelled curses. The campsite was littered with clothing, tools, and guns easily identifiable as to whom they belonged.

Only two natives were captured alive, a female and her baby daughter. The men were going to turn them over to Captain Bidwell in Chico, but the female committed suicide with a concealed pistol on the way. Hi Good, who was originally from Ohio, raised the child as his own. She grew up to be a bright little girl who spoke French, Spanish, and English. Good had some business to take care of in Idaho and left the child with an old sheepherder friend who was married to a native. Tragically, the little girl got sick and died while he was away.

Hi Good was greatly admired in Northern California as a defender of white people and a killer of Indians. It was reported that at one time Good had a collection of forty native scalps hanging on a poplar tree outside of his home.

On May 4, 1870, Good was murdered by a young native called Ned, whom Good had employed as a sheepherder and cook. Good was thirty-four years old when he was gunned down in a remote canyon. Ned was quickly caught when Good's friends notice that Ned was wearing Good's gold ring. He was led out to a tree and shot. His bones were left exposed for two years.

In those days, nobody bothered to ask or find out what the Mill Creek Indians called themselves. Nor did anyone inquire about their culture. Their history is lost to us and we will never know anything about them.

CHAPTER 3

The Evilest Stepmother

Gridley, Butte County
June 26, 1911

Emma Rumball was the quintessential evil stepmother. Her husband, William, suddenly died of unknown causes in September 1910, and left joint ownership of his thirty-acre farm and orchard near the Butte County town of Gridley to his thirteen-year-old daughter, Helen.

It was well known to the people of Gridley that twenty-four-year-old Emma and her brother, twenty-five-year-old Arthur Lewis, often brutalized the young teenager. Her schoolteacher once asked Helen about a black eye that she had; Helen told the teacher that her step-uncle Arthur Lewis had punched her in her face. In those days, before child protection agencies and laws against domestic violence, nothing was done for the poor girl.

Things finally came to a head on June 26, 1911, when Emma angrily alleged that Helen had milked only two of their three cows that morning and lied about it. Emma struck Helen until she became unconscious and then carried her up to the attic of her home. In the sweltering attic, Emma hogtied and hung the young girl from the rafters. To make sure that Helen would suffer, Emma also put a noose around her neck and pulled it taut. It was one of the hottest days of 1911, and a simmering egg incubator in the attic made it even more uncomfortable.

When Helen's sister, Francis, became upset about Helen's cries of pain, Emma chastised the girl and sent her to bed. Later that day, Emma's brother Arthur came over to the house and when told about the milking incident, he went up to the attic to taunt her. Nobody really knows what he did to the poor girl, but by eight o'clock that night, Helen was dead.

Emma told the neighbors that Helen had committed suicide, but they had heard her cries and did not believe her. The police were called, and Arthur and Emma were arrested.

At Arthur Lewis' trial in Oroville, witnesses testified that Lewis loved to show off his ability to break a steer's neck with a single twist. Lewis claimed that Helen had strangled herself while trying to free herself from the ropes that bound her. The coroner's report stated that Helen died from a double dislocation of vertebrae in her neck. The injury could not have happened by hanging.

Lewis was convicted of manslaughter and sentenced to seven years in prison. Emma Rumball was convicted in a separate trial and was sentenced to only two years in prison. Helen was laid to rest next to her father.

CHAPTER 4

The Wheatland Hop Riot

Wheatland, Yuba County
August 3, 1913

The summer of 1913 was one of the hottest summers in California history. On July 10, the thermometer hit 134 degrees Fahrenheit in Death Valley, the hottest recorded temperature in the history of the United States. The Sacramento Valley was as hot as a pizza oven, but the stifling heat didn't discourage thousands of agricultural workers who trekked to the vast hop fields of the Sacramento Valley to work the three-week harvest. Little did the temporary workers know just how hot the hop fields were going to be.

Hops are a creeping flower used as a flavoring and stability agent in beer. There is no major commercial use for the plant other than in the production of beer. A close relative of hemp, hops are grown on specially prepared fences and reach up to thirty feet in height by harvest time. Only the female flowers are harvested. Before mechanization, hop harvesting was a labor-intensive and dirty job, and the harvest season has only a three- to four-week window. The hop farmers hired as many workers as possible to ensure that the harvest was brought in on time, and the wages were kept low. Pickers worked from sunrise to sunset and sometimes even at night.

In 1913, the largest hop farm in the world was the Durst Brothers Hop Yard outside of Wheatland in Yuba County. The Durst Brothers knew their business well and had long arranged that their 640 acres of hops be sold to a single brewer in England. Only the finest hop cones were picked at the Durst Brothers farm. The drying and packaging were done on-site in hop kilns, and the product was transported on special trains to ships docked in the San Francisco Bay for the long voyage to England. The Durst Brothers were, at the time, the single largest employer of agricultural workers in the state.

The Durst Brothers had hired a German foreman who had new ideas on how to streamline production and maximize profit. The first thing he did was to get rid of the high pole men. The high pole men were young and athletic men who climbed thirty feet to the top of the hop vines to detach the vines from the support fence for the pickers below. The high pole men's other duties were to carry, weigh, and load the hops onto a wagon. As a result of this cost-cutting process, women and children had to reach the hops, no matter how high they were. The pickers then had to carry their own hopsacks, which generally weighed one hundred pounds, to the scales and then load the sacks onto the transport wagon. This lessened the time that the worker could be picking, thus earning money.

If climbing thirty feet up rickety poles, hauling, weighing, and loading hundred pound sacks wasn't enough, the Durst Brothers also saved money by not providing fresh water to their workers in the fields. Instead, they charged five cents a glass for a mixture of water and acetic acid. Food had to be bought at Durst's company store, where the costs were high and the quality low. The sanitary conditions at the Durst Yards camp were nonexistent. The water in the nearby irrigation canals was contaminated and undrinkable. There were only nine doorless outhouses provided at the workers camp and none were provided in the fields. Garbage was tossed into ditches and irrigation canals. Dysentery quickly spread through the dusty campground. In the one-hundred degree heat, the stench was appalling.

In order to keep the pickers for the entire eighteen- to twenty-day harvest, the Durst Brothers inaugurated a bonus system that was only a bonus to the brothers. The going rate for picking hops in 1913 was one dollar for every one hundred

Hop picking was a hot, dirty and exhausting job. *California State Library*

pounds of hops. The Durst Brothers paid only ninety cents per one hundred pounds on the first week. During the second week, the pickers received a dollar per hundred pounds picked, and during the third week they received one dollar and ten cents per hundred pounds picked. This system was employed to keep the pickers at the Durst Yards for the entire season. It was estimated that the Durst Brothers profited a hundred dollars a day in wage holdbacks forfeited by pickers who left before the season was over.

On August 1, approximately three thousand people signed up to work the 1913 harvest at the Durst Ranch, about twice as many as needed, as the drying ovens at the Durst Yards only had the capacity to process the output of 1,500 pickers a day. Ranch manager Ralph H. Durst was following the common practice of advertising for more workers than he really needed to ensure that the crop was brought in on time.

By the second day of the harvest, 1,700 workers held an informal meeting in the evening. There were more than twenty-five different nationalities working at the Durst Yards, along with a couple dozen members of the Industrial Workers of the World, also known as Wobblies. Among the I.W.W. members was Richard Blackie Ford, an articulate and experienced organizer. A grievance committee was formed and leaders were elected to notify Ralph Durst of their demands for a flat rate of one dollar twenty-five cents per one hundred pounds of hops. They would also demand fresh ice water in the fields three times a day, sanitary toilets, garbage collection, and the rehiring of the high pole men.

The next day, the grievance committee, led by Blackie Ford, along with four to five hundred pickers and thirty battle-experienced Wobblies, assembled at the dance platform a half a mile from the company office and marched in columns of four to the hop yard's headquarters. When Durst came out of his office, the marchers called themselves to a halt and the grievance was read to Durst. To his credit, Durst listened to the demands and asked for an hour to think it over. The grievance committee gave him two hours.

Ralph Durst, the rat-faced, derby-wearing, cigar-chomping manager of the yard, halfheartedly agreed to all of the demands except for the wage increase. When told by Ford that there would be a strike, Durst charged at him and slapped him across the face with a heavy work glove. He then ordered him and the other marchers off his property. They refused to leave.

Durst went off to Wheatland to get the police and his attorney Edmund Tecumseh Manwell, who just happened to be the district attorney of Yuba County. Manwell, along with Yuba County sheriff George H. Voss and constables L. B. Anderson, Elmer Bradshaw, Henry Daken and Eugene Reardon, joined Ralph Durst to evict the protesters. Sheriff Voss had deputized Anderson, Daken, and Reardon before they drove out to the Durst Yards. Reardon was a sixty-seven-year-old sheep shearer from Red Bluff, who in his younger days was a renowned Indian fighter. He was on his way to work in Sutter County when Sheriff Voss asked him to join the posse.

The posse spotted the protesters at the dance platform and roared up in their auto to confront them. Firing his pistol into the air for emphasis, Voss yelled to the crowd, "I'm the sheriff of Yuba County! Disperse!" But the workers stood their ground and one of them threw a rock, striking Sheriff Voss in the head. Walking through the crowd, the authorities nervously eyed the protesters milling about the dance floor, when Ralph Durst suddenly spotted Blackie Ford. Durst pointed at Ford and yelled to the posse, "That's the man! Take him!" As the officers grabbed Ford, the crowd surged forward and all hell broke loose.

The crowd grabbed Sheriff Voss, took his weapons and beat him to the ground, as Deputy Daken fired his sawed-off shotgun into the air. Deputy Reardon pulled out his pistol, but an African-American picker grabbed his arm and grappled with the old Indian killer. The gun went off wildly several

Dozens of mule drawn wagons get ready to collect hops in the hot August heat. *California State Library*

times as the men struggled. Finally, the striker wrenched the pistol from Reardon's hand and beat him over the head with it. District Attorney Manwell rushed up to the fallen officers and was shot in the heart by the African-American worker. Conflicting articles in the *Sacramento Bee* said that Ralph Durst shot the African-American worker in the chest, creating a hole behind his left nipple large enough to drop a hen's egg into, but Deputy Daken later took credit for the kill. It is known that Durst and his guards fired indiscriminately into the crowd until their guns were empty. Jumping into their car, Durst and his goons retreated to the farmhouse, leaving the officers to fend for themselves. The crowd beat Deputy Daken until he broke away and ran for the company store. Once at the store, Daken shaved off his mustache, threw out his false teeth, and darkened his face to disguise himself from the searching rioters. Posing as a company bookkeeper, Daken fooled the mob and made his escape at sunset.

When the gunsmoke cleared, District Attorney Manwell, Deputy Reardon, the unidentified African-American and eighteen-year-old Sacramento picker Ed Donnelly, who apparently worked at a different hop farm and was an innocent bystander, all lay dead. Deputy Anderson received a severe scalp wound and was shot in the arm. Sheriff Voss was beaten bloody and left with a broken left leg. Deputy Bradshaw was shot in the elbow. Nels Nelson, a Durst goon, had his right arm shattered by a shotgun blast. It was reported that many of the protesters were injured, including two women and a boy who were secreted away by the pickers.

Fearing retribution, hundreds of Durst farm pickers packed up as fast as they could and scrambled away from the campground, seeking work at more humane hop yards or catching the first train out of Yuba County. The police put up a dragnet and caught Blackie Ford along with other suspected Wobblies. Fearing gangs of Wobblies from all over the West would descend on the hop farms of Yuba County, Governor Hiram W. Johnson called out the state's militia to keep the peace in Wheatland. The I.W.W. invasion never materialized and the militia was sent home by August 9.

Durst Brothers ended up giving in to the protesters' demands and fresh ice water was provided in the field, garbage was collected, more outhouses were provided in the campgrounds and in the fields, the use of high pole men was reinstituted, and the pickers were paid a flat rate of a dollar per hundred pounds.

Ford and another I.W.W. leader, Herman Suhr, who wasn't present at the riot, were eventually convicted of second-degree murder and sentenced to life imprisonment. The prosecutor admitted that Ford and Suhr had not taken part in the riot, but argued they were guilty of provoking workers into violence by being members of the I.W.W. Their highly publicized trial put a spotlight on the plight of the farm workers and many new, but generally ineffective laws were put into place to improve conditions to protect the workers. Ford and Suhr became labor martyrs and were pardoned in 1925.

Next to an electrical substation and almost surrounded by a chain link fence, a plaque set on a stone in Wheatland marks the location of the dance platform where the uprising occurred on that hot bloody Sunday. Dedicated in 1988, on the seventy-fifth anniversary of the unrest, by the Camp Far West Parlor Number 218 N.D.G.W.—Wheatland Historical Society—it states:

Durst Hop Ranch—Site of Wheatland Hop Riot
August 3, 1913
Second Major Labor Dispute in the U.S.A.
Initiated by the I.W.W. Labor Movement

It is one rare case in which the losers placed a monument acknowledging their responsibility and subsequent defeat.

CHAPTER 5

President Harding Is Dead

San Francisco
August 2, 1923

History has not been kind to the administration of Warren G. Harding, the 29th president of the United States of America. His tenure as the leader of America is littered with scandals, and had he not died under mysterious circumstances at the Palace Hotel in San Francisco, he would have no doubt been impeached.

Born on November 2, 1865, outside of Marion, Ohio, to a well-to-do family, Harding attended the now defunct Ohio Central College, where he studied printing and journalism. After college, he and some friends, with the help of his father, bought the ailing *Marion Daily Star*, one of Marion's three daily papers. Harding immediately started a war of words with the other two papers in Marion and saw the circulation of the *Daily Star* rise, but the toll of the circulation wars wore Harding out and he was admitted to the Battle Creek Sanitarium, the first of his multiple visits there.

In 1891, Harding married divorcee Florence Kling, the daughter of Amos Hall Kling, the owner of the *Marion Independent*. Florence, known as The Duchess to her husband and his friends because of her cold and haughty disposition, was five years older than Harding and lugged along a young son from her previous marriage. She had relentlessly pursued Harding for years, and Harding reluctantly married her.

Florence was a plain-looking woman, and her domineering personality didn't endear her to many people, but because of her management skills the twenty-six-year-old editor and publisher saw his *Daily Star* become an influential Ohio newspaper. With Florence running the paper, the handsome Harding had plenty of time for his favorite activities: playing cards with his buddies and hobnobbing with the people of Marion.

Harding, a gifted public speaker, eventually entered politics as an Ohio state senator and served from 1899 to 1903. He was elected lieutenant governor and served from 1904 to 1906, and then ran on the Republican ticket for governor in 1910, but was defeated in the general election by Democrat Judson Harmon. Harding became a United States senator from Ohio in 1915.

Known to everyone in Marion, Ohio, except for Florence, Harding was having a torrid affair with Carrie Phillips, the wife of his friend, Jim Phillips. Florence finally learned of the affair in 1914, nine years after the relationship started, and she was infuriated by the news. More than once, Florence chased Carrie off her property and she was known to shake her fist at her when she spotted Carrie in the audience at her husband's campaign speeches.

In 1911, after it was clear that Harding would not divorce his wife, Carrie went to Germany to live. She continued to correspond with Harding and encouraged him to vote pro-German in the Senate. She returned to America in 1914 and continued to lobby Harding to stay neutral or to side with Germany during dealings in the Senate.

The relationship lasted until 1920, when Harding started eyeing higher office. Carrie and Jim were paid $20,000 and expenses to go on an extended vacation abroad with the stipulation that they stay outside of the United States until

Harding left office. They came back to America after Harding's death.

Harding's fondness for extramarital affairs didn't stop with Carrie Phillips. Nan Britton was the daughter of a family friend of the Hardings who had an adolescent crush on the middle-aged politician beginning in 1910, going as far as pasting campaign pictures of her heartthrob on her bedroom walls. In 1917, she mailed Senator Harding a letter asking if he could help her find a job. Harding traveled from Washington to New York City to visit the twenty-one-year-old beauty and immediately began a sexual relationship with her. He also got her a secretary job at U.S. Steel's headquarters in New York City.

After Harding became the 29th president of the United States in 1921, the lovebirds continued their affair right under the nose of the dour Florence. Secret Service agents snuck Nan into the White House at all hours of the day and warned the couple when Florence was approaching. Their favorite make-out spot in the White House was in a closet in the Oval Office. Nan became pregnant and gave birth to Harding's child, Elizabeth Ann, on October 22, 1919, and although he never saw the baby, he paid a large amount each month for child support.

But Harding's problems were bigger that a couple of love affairs and an illegitimate child. From the start of his political career, Harding was backed by men of dubious morals, and he appointed some of them to positions of power in his cabinet. Called the Ohio Gang, the men were the Republican movers and shakers of the Buckeye State and they knew no bounds when it came to corruption. To make sure that the Ohio Gang would be able to plunder the U.S. Treasury without repercussions, Ohio Republican Party boss Harry Daugherty was installed as attorney general. The Ohio Gang's main interest was to give government contracts and oil leases to their business associates in exchange for bribes.

Charles Forbes, the director of the Veterans Bureau, skimmed money from the budget, took bribes, and ran a drug and alcohol smuggling operation. The Veterans Bureau was created by Harding to take care of the thousands of returning World War I veterans. The head of the Office of Alien Property, Thomas W. Miller, was convicted of bribery, and Jesse Smith, the personal aide to the attorney general, burned documents that would have incriminated himself and others before he committed suicide.

The largest of these scandals occurred when Secretary of the Interior Albert B. Fall got his friends, oilmen Harry F. Sinclair and Edward L. Doheny, a no-bid contract to the naval oil reserves in Elk Hills and Buena Vista, California, and Teapot Dome, Wyoming, for a bribe of $385,000. Fall became the first member of a presidential cabinet to go to jail for crimes while in office.

While these scandals were being investigated and uncovered, Harding, who either knew, or was too naïve or stupid to know, that his trusted cabinet was involved in corruption, decided that the summer of 1923 would be a good time to leave the District of Columbia for a goodwill railroad tour of the United States.

Calling the trip a Voyage of Understanding, Harding wanted to rub elbows with regular people and explain his policies in a few speeches in the hinterlands of America. Traveling in a luxurious Pullman coach, Harding and the First Lady journeyed as far as Alaska to get away from the media and the Democratic members of the Congress. But while in Alaska, Harding received a long message outlining the crimes of his friends, whom he had trusted. Harding was apparently shocked by the news, and he quickly realized that most members of his administration were going to be indicted and he would be impeached.

Harding became gravely ill on his way back from Alaska, apparently from food poisoning. He planned stops in Seattle,

Portland, and San Francisco, but Harding cancelled the Portland stop after giving a speech at the University of Washington in Seattle and traveled on to San Francisco.

Exhausted, Harding was taken to the Palace Hotel, to which more doctors were summoned. After a couple of days, Harding appeared to be better and by August 2, he seemed to have completely recovered from his illness. He and the Duchess spent the evening alone until she retired to her room across the hall. The nurse entered Harding's suite minutes after Mrs. Harding left, just in time to see the President's head shiver and drop.

President Harding was declared dead by Dr. Joel Boone, the vice admiral of the United States Naval Medical Corps. Along with Harding's personal physician, Charles Sawyer, and three other physicians, he declared that the cause of death was probably apoplexy. At Mrs. Harding's and Dr. Sawyer's request, no autopsy was performed, and Harding was embalmed at the hotel.

Immediately afterward, rumors popped up that the President had been poisoned, but with the quick embalming and lack of an autopsy, there was little that anyone could do. Many important people depended on Harding keeping his mouth shut and likely would not have been beyond killing the President to keep themselves out of prison.

Mrs. Harding was also suspected of killing the President, as she was the last person with him before he died, and she had put up with his infidelities their entire married life to see him become the leader of the free world. Without Florence's ambition and guidance, Harding would have never achieved such political heights. Now she saw the handwriting on the wall and realized that her husband's career was going to end in disgrace. Could she have poisoned him to protect him from the embarrassment of impeachment and possibly prison, or did she finally take revenge on him for a lifetime of infidelities? Harding's personal physician, Charles

Sawyer, died thirteen months later and Mrs. Harding passed away from a longtime kidney aliment on November 21, 1924, a little more than a year after her husband's death.

Unless Warren G. Harding is exhumed and tested for traces of toxins, as President Zachary Taylor was in 1991 (he was found free of any toxins that could have killed him), nobody will ever know what really killed the robust fifty-seven-year-old president.

The body of President Warren G. Harding leaving the Palace Hotel in San Francisco.
California State Library

CHAPTER 6

Vernal Fall 14/Humans 0

Yosemite National Park

California is blessed with extensive natural beauty, and one of the most beautiful places on Earth is Yosemite National Park. A World Heritage Site since 1984, Yosemite was the first parcel of land to be designated for protection by the federal government on June 30, 1864, by President Abraham Lincoln. The State of California controlled the area until it was transferred to the National Park Service on its inception in 1916.

Millions of tourists have visited Yosemite over the years to enjoy its breathtaking mountain vistas, cascading waterfalls, and 800 miles of hiking trails. It has been said that you can walk fifty yards from any of the park's roads and you will be in the wilderness. This extent of wilderness is why it is so easy for a tragedy to occur in the park. There are 704,624 acres of land in Yosemite and 92.4 percent of that is wilderness. Add over 3.5 million visitors each year and the odds are that someone is going to die there.

The most deadly single place in Yosemite National Park is Vernal Fall, where the Merced River tumbles 317 feet into a pool of rocks and boulders. As of 2006, fourteen people have fallen over its ledge. None of them survived.

The first recorded death at Vernal Fall was sixteen-year-old Lucille Duling, who stepped into the abyss on August 22, 1924. Lucille was enjoying her vacation at Yosemite National Park, a giant change of scenery from that of her life in Hollywood, which was then a dusty town of orchards mixed with the emerging film industry. After a grueling climb to the head of Vernal Fall, Lucille, along with her father and her friend Riva Straub, stopped to admire the magnificent waterfall that plunges 317 feet out of the Sierra Nevada Mountains. The teenagers posed for photos by the guardrail, but the girls thought that they could get a more dramatic photo if they were on the other side of the River of Our Lady of Mercy.

Being late summer, the river was running deceptively low and the girls had no difficulty getting across the river for their photos. Riva crossed the river without a problem, while Lucille's father changed the film in his camera. Lucille took a different route than Riva and started to jump from rock to rock. Perhaps she slipped on the algae-covered smooth river rocks or maybe the ice-cold water numbed her feet too much; whatever the case, the teenage girl fell into the river and disappeared, only to surface in time to scream as she plummeted over the ledge to her death.

The panic-stricken father ran down the trail to the base of the falls, while Riva ran to get a ranger. Lucille's lifeless body bobbed violently around in the pool, as her father tried desperately to swim out to his daughter. They retrieved her later with a rope. Lucille Duling was the first waterfall fatality in Yosemite, the result of a failed photo opportunity. Unfortunately, she wasn't the last.

On June 29, 1929, a twelve-year-old boy from Burlingame was enthralled by the spectacular view while standing in the middle of the Merced River. Forest Case and his friend Edward Shoemaker had hiked up the Mist Trail to the top of the falls. Case stepped about twenty feet into the river after getting a drink of water. He shouted to Shoemaker, "Look at those mountains up there, with the white clouds floating around them!" Those were his last words as he lost his footing and fell into the swift current.

Shoemaker ran to help his struggling friend and got as close as grabbing Case's hand, but the river tore their death grip apart and Case went screaming over the falls in front of dozens of witnesses. Three female witnesses fainted at the sight of the boy falling over the ledge. Case's body was never found.

Orville Dale Loos was on leave from the U.S. Navy when he and two other sailors went to visit Yosemite. Loos, a native of Dayton, Ohio, was hiking along the top edge of Vernal Fall when he saw eleven-year old Keen Freeman being carried down the river toward the lip of the falls. The boy and his father, Dr. Walter Freeman, were visiting the park from Washington, D.C. Keen had fallen into the river while trying to fill his canteen. The sailors jumped the guardrail to try to save the boy from a certain death. Loos got ahead of the other rescuers and was able to grab Freeman just fifteen feet from the brink. Swimming against the powerful current with Freeman under his arm, Loos made it to a finely polished boulder and clung on for a few seconds before the algae-covered rock made him lose his grip, and both Freeman and Loos were swept to their deaths. Freeman's body was found a week later. Loos was found five days after Freeman, just a hundred yards from the base of the falls.

The next three deaths at Vernal Fall happened without any witnesses. William C. Hansch apparently went off the trail on June 3, 1947. The forty-year-old man from Sacramento had left his backpack near the top of the falls and his body was found fifty-four days later at the base. On August 8, 1965, twelve-year-old Ohioan Daniel R. Duda mysteriously went over Vernal Fall and was not found until October 16. Seven-year-old Roberta Mary Hurd of Jackson was on a family vacation in Yosemite, when, while her parents were momentarily distracted, she fell into the river. She was spotted by a witness just as she was about to go over the falls. She was found on July 4.

On June 18, 1970, tragedy again struck Vernal Fall. After climbing over barriers and ignoring signs warning hikers not to go into the Merced River, thirty-year-old La Puente resident Yolanda Fuentes and her daughter Christine, along with five other members of their party, sat on the rocks in the raging river to cool off and take photos, less than sixty feet from the lip of the falls. A woman who was standing in the water taking photos dropped her hat into the water. Little Christine sloshed over to retrieve it and was pulled into the strong current. Her mother Yolanda chased after her daughter and was gripped by the rushing water. One by one, the hat, Christine, and Yolanda were all swept over the ledge to their deaths. Yolanda's decomposed body was found over two months later. Christine's body was never found.

William Ramirez of Gardena hiked up the Mist Trail with his brother John on July 11, 1971. Hot and sweaty from the hike in the summer heat, William climbed over the guardrail to take a dip in the cool waters of the Merced River. John wisely stayed on shore and expressed his concern to his brother about the wisdom of swimming in the water despite all the signs warning against it. William ignored his brother and continued to swim 175 feet upstream of the rim. The current snatched him and pulled him downstream. Witnesses said that Ramirez appeared to be in shock and made no effort to struggle out of the death ride. John ran into the river to save his brother but realized that he too would be dragged over the falls and got out. William Ramirez was found by hikers ten days later.

Nine days later, sixteen-year-old Randy Friedman was with a tour group viewing the natural beauty of Yosemite National Park. The Hartsdale, New York, teenager climbed over the guardrail to fill his canteen, and before anyone could comprehend what had happened, Friedman went over the brink; his body was never found.

Vernal Fall was the site of at least one apparent suicide when on April 30, 1973, Leah Oliver Good told her husband, a park assistant superintendent, that she was going for a hike. The next day hikers found her body fifty yards from the base of the falls. She had died from the impact of falling 317 feet. The forty-nine-year-old Good was sick with cancer and had probably committed suicide.

Fresno native David Kingseng Chu hiked up the Mist Trail with his family on August 18, 1977. After the ascent, Chu climbed over the guardrail festooned with warning signs and waded into the icy Merced River just twelve feet from the lip of the killer waterfall.

The river was running low and 1977 was a drought year; however, gravity trumps stupidity. Chu wanted to take a photograph of the water falling over its ledge, standing in the middle and on the very tip of the falls. Realizing the danger that was upon him, he panicked and leaped sideways toward a nearby dry boulder. Slipping on the algae-covered river boulders that lay just below the surface, Chu's feet came out from under him and he disappeared over the edge.

The Yosemite Search and Rescue (SAR) team arrived and unsuccessfully searched the boulder-strewn basin. They sent searchers downstream to search for the body, but to no avail. Rangers believed that Chu's body may have been stuck in a crevasse behind the pounding wall of water.

The next day, the SAR team sent in a wetsuit-clad ranger seventy-five feet from the bottom of the falls. Dangling from safety ropes, the ranger worked his way sideways into the falls. The freezing water easily pierced the neoprene-insulated suit and the force of the falling water at times almost drowned him. After staying as long as he could, he was replaced by another ranger who brought along a seven-foot fireman's pike.

The ranger found Chu's crushed body wedged four feet into an eighteen-inch-wide crevice.

Twenty-eight years went by before the next death occurred at Vernal Fall, when Silicon Valley software engineer Chintan Dakshehbai Chokshi made a decision that would cost him his life. The twenty-four-year-old native of Ahmedabad, India, was with a group of friends on their way to Nevada Fall and stopped to rest at Vernal Fall. Wanting to wash his face in the cold Merced River, Chokshi climbed over the barrier rail and unknowingly walked towards his death. Stepping into the river, Chokshi immediately slipped on the slick rocks, fell on his butt, and was pulled into the current. While struggling desperately to regain his footing, Chokshi was pulled to his death.

Chokshi's body was discovered on September 24, and to add to the tragedy, National Park Service special agent Dan Madrid suffered a fatal asthma attack while participating in the recovery of the body.

The tranquility of nature can turn to real danger in a heartbeat.

CHAPTER 7

The Ape Boy

Wineville/Mira Loma, Riverside County
1926 to 1928

At first the detectives of the Los Angeles County Sheriff's Department couldn't believe the tales that fourteen-year-old Canadian Sanford Clark was telling them. At the request of the American consulate in Vancouver, Canada, the detectives picked up the teenager to look into his well-being. His sister was concerned about him after she had visited him at their cousin's chicken ranch in Wineville, a small hamlet located in the northeast corner of Riverside County.

Clark told police that he had been kidnapped from his home in Saskatchewan in 1926 and was kept at the decrepit ranch against his will. He breathlessly told the investigators tales of kidnapping, rape, torture, and murder, all committed by his uncle, twenty-one-year-old Gordon Stewart Northcott. He claimed that his uncle threatened to kill him if he told authorities about the happenings at the farm.

The Los Angeles County Sheriff's Department contacted the Riverside County Sheriff's Department, and the two teams jointly inspected the now-abandoned ranch. Investigators quickly lost their skepticism as well as their lunches. The run-down, three-acre compound on the edge of the desert was definitely a crime scene. Police found bloodstained stairs, cots, a bloody axe, a hatchet imbedded with human hair, a blood-stained bucket, and three recently exhumed, gore-soaked, shallow graves. One of the quicklime-lined graves had the imprints of two small bodies in the dirt at the bottom, while the other had an impression of one small body. Bone fragments were scattered all over the ranch and surrounding area, and many of them were obviously human. Most incriminating of all were articles of clothing that were easily traced to three recently missing boys and an unidentified teenage body found in nearby Norco.

Nine-year-old Walter Collins had gone to see a movie on March 10, 1928, and never returned. Tattered remnants of his clothing were found in what turned out to have been Northcott's torture room. It was in this room where Collins—along with brothers Lewis and Nelson Winslow, who were last seen on May 16—were subjected to sexual assault, sadistic beatings, and finally death. Clark told the police that Northcott had either lured the boys to the death ranch with a promise of work or just plain kidnapped them. His ape-like uncle then overpowered them, tore their clothes off, and tied them face down on a cot, where he raped and tortured them for a week before he tired of them.

The infamous Wineville Chicken Ranch. *Los Angeles County Library*

Sanford Clark pointed out everything to the detectives. He told them that there was at least one other boy killed at the ranch while he was enslaved there, a Hispanic teenager who was raped and tortured for a week before he was shot and decapitated. Northcott made Clark carry his decapitated head to a shed in the blood-stained bucket.

The first to die in front of Clark was the Hispanic boy, who had been hiding near a miner's cabin in the Mint Valley. Northcott knew a miner who lived there and would often go visit him. One day the miner's partner showed up and the two men argued over profits. Northcott gladly helped his miner friend kill his partner. While the men looked for a convenient hole to throw the hapless prospector into, they found the Hispanic boy hiding in an old mineshaft. Believing that the boy had seen the murder, Northcott took him back to his ranch and raped, beat, and tortured him for a week, before the miner came back to the ranch and allegedly murdered the hapless teen with a .22 caliber rifle that was also found at the ranch. His head was chopped off to forestall identification.

The police knew about a headless torso of a Hispanic teenager that had been found on February 2 alongside the road outside of the nearby community of Norco; there was a .22 caliber bullet wound in the body, which was never identified.

Clark told the police that he had originally dug the two graves for a married couple who were interested in working at the ranch. The couple, known as the Dahls, went to the ranch, but became frightened after they were asked to wait on the front porch of the house while Northcott and his mother, Sarah Louisa Northcott, argued. After listening to the quarreling couple for two hours, the couple quietly got into their car and left.

The police put out an all-points-bulletin for the capture of Gordon, his mother, and his father. Not long after putting

Clark into protective custody, police arrested Gordon's sixty-four-year-old father, Cyrus George Northcott, in Los Angeles.

The elderly Northcott couldn't keep his mouth shut while being interrogated, telling investigators that he moved from Canada to California to get away from his family, but they found out where he was and moved in with him. The old carpenter claimed that his son told him about the murders, but he said he didn't believe anything Gordon said. The old man told the police that his wife and son attempted to kill him several times, the last attempt occurring just a month earlier.

Cyrus called his son an ape man, claiming that Gordon's body was covered with three-inch-long hair. The press jumped on the nickname and from there on always referred to Gordon as Ape Boy in the headlines.

Cyrus and Sarah bought the ranch for Gordon to keep him out of trouble. In 1925, Gordon had been reprimanded by a judge for an unnamed statutory offense with a twelve-year-old boy. Love letters found on the ranch revealed that the boy was the child of an elderly and wealthy resident of the old-money Los Angeles neighborhood known as Highland Park. The police would not disclose the name of the person or the child. More importantly, Cyrus told police that his son would drive into Los Angeles and go from door to door asking young teenage males if they wanted to earn some money working on his farm. The old man had no idea how many people his son had waylaid and murdered in this way. He told the police that he may have taken many of his victims to the miner's cabin in the Mint Canyon.

Riverside County sheriff Clem Sweeters and his investigators combed through the isolated chicken ranch, finding more human bone fragments and a kneecap. All were from the bodies of adolescent males. The police believed that the graves had been dug up and the bodies torn apart. A buzzard circling a few hundred feet away from the ranch caught

Gordon Northcott, murderer and rapist of young boys, signs out of LAPD custody. *Los Angeles County Library*

the attention of the searchers. There officers found a blood-stained flour sack with two human pelvises inside.

A search of the miner's cabin in Mint Valley would yield more gruesome artifacts like fragments of ankles, fingers, toes, and leg bones. A piece of human skull was also sifted from the dirt. In a fire pit, the police found the remains of shoes.

Walter Collins' father identified tattered remains of cloth-ing as those of his son, which put the Los Angeles County Sheriff's Department in a dilemma. Arthur Hutchins, Jr., a twelve-year-old runaway from Iowa, had tricked the po-lice into believing that he was nine-year-old Walter Collins. When he was picked up in Illinois, the police asked him if he was Collins. Wanting to get a free trip to California, Hutchins pretended that he was the missing boy. When Walter's moth-er, Christine Collins, was shown the boy, she immediately told Captain J. J. Jones that it wasn't her son. To placate the despondent mother, Captain Jones told her to try him out for a couple of weeks.

After three weeks, Christine Collins went to the police station with her son's dental and medical records to prove that Hutchins was not her son. Captain Jones responded by institutionalizing Mrs. Collins in a mental hospital. She was released after ten days, when her son's clothing was discovered and identified. Arthur Hutchins, Jr. was sent back to the Iowa authorities.

Sarah Louisa Northcott was captured without incident in Calgary, Alberta, Canada, and shipped off to Vancouver for extradition. Gordon Northcott, who was thought to be traveling disguised as a female, was captured at almost the same time in Vernon, British Columbia, Canada. Gordon Northcott began a process of grandstanding to the media that would continue throughout his trial. A tall and ungainly man, Northcott could look like a serious college student one moment and a mentally defective person the next. The lipstick-wearing killer couldn't keep his mouth shut and denied all charges against him. While in custody, Northcott told so many stories that the court believed that he was preparing to plead insanity. He said that he would fight extradition, but the Canadian authorities had no problem turning over the demented couple to California police and Gordon found himself on a long train ride, sandwiched between two burly detectives from the Riverside County Sheriff's Department.

Sarah Northcott, shriveled and hideous, looked far older than her sixty years. Her deep love for her son bordered on insanity. She wanted to take the blame for all the murders, but she ended up being convicted of the murder of Walter Collins, through the testimony of her grandson, Sanford Clark. The teenager had witnessed his grandmother axing the Collins boy in the head while he was tied down to the gore-crusted cot. In one of the quickest trials in Riverside

County history, Sarah was sentenced on December 31, 1928, to life in the Tehachapi State Prison.

It is a timeworn anecdote that a person who represents himself in court has a fool for an attorney. One of the first things that Northcott did when his trial started was to fire his attorneys. The demented killer believed that he was smart enough to get himself acquitted on his own. Plus, acting as his own attorney gave Northcott freedom of movement around the jail and access to interview witnesses in private. Thus began one of the most bizarre and confusing trials in California history.

Northcott wasted the court's time by requesting a change in venue, demanding more females on the jury, and subpoenaing over sixty people, including Christine Collins, the mother of Walter Collins and the victim of police brutality when she was locked up in a mental ward for trying to prove that Arthur Hutchins, Jr. was not her son. The only thing that Northcott accomplished was to get the original judge disqualified.

Northcott loved the attention he was receiving, and when advised by an attorney that he would hang himself by acting in this own defense, Northcott replied, "Well, it would be worth it. My name will become known all over the world."

The trial started on January 15, 1929, and was presided over by the Honorable George Freeman. Judge Freeman did the best he could to conceal his loathing for Northcott and proceeded with as fair a trial as a maniac like Northcott could receive.

Special Prosecutor Loyal C. Kelly put Sanford Clark on the stand, and he testified that Gordon had him dig three graves that were originally for the Dahls. He described how the boys were brought to the ranch, stripped, and tied down onto filthy cots in the shed. In detail, he put into plain words how Northcott would rape, beat, and torture the poor boys until he tired of them, which usually took about a week. He'd then whack the poor kid in the head with his axe. He told the court how Northcott, under the threat of death, made him hit Lewis Winslow in the head with a double-bladed axe in front of the grave that he had dug earlier. He reported to the court that he saw his uncle carrying a bucket with the Mexican boy's head in it. One of the most heartbreaking moments during the trial was when it was exposed that Northcott made the tortured Winslow boys write a letter to their parents explaining that they ran away from home. Clark testified that as soon as the boys were done with the letters, they were killed. He also told the court about how they dug up the bodies and that Northcott told him that he reburied the bodies fifty miles out in the desert.

When cross-examined, Clark held his own against his evil uncle's inane questioning. Northcott jutted his jaw and

Sanford Clark poses with detectives and a flour sack, much like the one that held the head of the Mexican teenager that his Uncle Gordon killed. *Los Angeles County Library*

made theatrical gestures, but he could not jar the teenager's testimony.

The detectives were on the stand next, and the amount of evidence against Northcott was overwhelming—bloody clothing that was identified by the families of the missing boys, murder weapons, and Northcott's own confession, which he had recklessly blurted out to his jailers while incarcerated. Northcott turned pale when the confession was read in court. The entry as evidence of a couple of bushel baskets of human bone fragments raked up from his ranch did not help his case.

Gordon Northcott poses for the camera. *Los Angeles County Library*

Northcott's sister, niece, father, and mother were brought in to testify, and their testimony did nothing to help his case. Cyrus told him to just admit that he was guilty. Sarah Northcott, more pasty faced and drawn-looking than before she went to prison, could only cry on the stand. She told the court between sobs that she was guilty of all the crimes, but nobody believed her, and she was quickly led back to prison.

Northcott's sister Winnie Clark was brought in from Canada at the state's expense for the defendant's case, only to be accused by Northcott of being his mother. Eventually the truth came out that Gordon Northcott was the product of an incestuous relationship between his father Cyrus and Winnie. His father was also his grandfather. Although shocking, the revelation didn't help his case.

It didn't go well for Northcott as he asked his niece, Sarah Clark, questions that only incriminated himself. A fine example of Northcott's idiotic defense happened when he asked Winnie how she knew that he gave her a black eye. "Because you punched me in the eye with your fist," she replied.

Gordon Northcott's trial ended with him questioning himself, turning his head one way when questioning and the other way when answering. He ended up pleading for his life.

The jury was taken to the Chicken Ranch and given a tour. They saw the bloody steps that led to the killing room. They saw the room where the boys were tortured. They saw the empty graves.

The twenty-seven-day trial ended when the jury came back with the guilty verdict after deliberating for less than two and a half hours. Gordon Northcott was sentenced to death by hanging.

The trial enraged the citizens of Riverside County. On February 10, a mob approached the jail and demanded to be allowed to lynch Northcott. Sheriff Clem Sweeters calmly talked the men out of it and sent them on their way. Before that, on January 2, 1929, Henry Espazo went to the Riverside County jail and asked to visit Northcott. Suspicious deputies frisked the country store shopkeeper and found a semi-automatic pistol. He was arrested for being an alien with a firearm.

After the usual appeals and legal tricks ran out, Gordon Northcott was still psychotically confident. He didn't let up on his shenanigans. He taunted officials about more bodies and sent them on wild goose chases. On his last evening, he agreed to meet with Christine Collins to answer any questions that she may have about the death of her son, Walter. It was the only time a woman was ever allowed into a death row jail cell in San Quentin's history. But Northcott was his usual glib self and only told her to ask his mother, father, or Sanford Clark for information.

An hour before Northcott was to be executed on October 2, 1930, he told the warden that he had taken poison to beat the rope. They immediately pumped his stomach but found no traces of any kind of poison.

The Ape Boy's playful and unrealistic self-confidence changed as he was led from his death row cell to the gallows of San Quentin. He was so nervous about his execution that he had to be blindfolded for his dead man's stroll. He was the first man to be blindfolded before he stood on the gallows in San Quentin history. On the short walk, he collapsed and had to be supported by two guards.

As the noose was being adjusted around his neck, Northcott uttered his last words.

"Don't, don't," he said pathetically.

Northcott fainted just as the trapdoor was sprung and the slack rope failed to break his neck. It took thirteen minutes for the Ape Boy to strangle to death.

The aftermath of the terrible crimes reverberated throughout the country. The town of Wineville was so embarrassed by the attention that it received from Northcott and the murders that on November 1, 1930, its name was changed to Mira Loma. The authorities were sure that there were at least twenty other Northcott victims buried out in the desert or thrown down an abandoned mineshaft. Anxious parents with missing children demanded that the police check out every lead.

In 2008, Clint Eastwood directed the film *Changeling*, starring Angelina Jolie and John Malkovich. The film focused on Christine Collins, her search for her son and the abuse that she suffered at the hands of the police.

Sarah Northcott was released from prison after serving only twelve years of her sentence. She slipped into obscurity as had the bodies of her grandson's victims.

CHAPTER 8

Russ Columbo

Los Angeles
September 2, 1934

Rarely has a singer and actor had such a meteoritic rise to fame, only to have his life cut short by a bizarre accident before his talents peaked, as did Russ Columbo. The youngest of twelve children, Colombo was born Ruggerio Eugenio di Rodolpho Columbo to Italian immigrants Nicola and Guilai Columbo, in Camden, New Jersey, on January 14, 1908.

Columbo's family moved often during his younger years, with stretches in Philadelphia, San Francisco, Calistoga, and finally Los Angeles, purportedly so young Ruggerio could keep taking singing lessons from *Phantom of the Opera* star Alexander Bevani. Russ made his professional debut at the Imperial Theater in San Francisco at the age of thirteen. While spending his high school years in Los Angeles, he was the first violinist in the Belmont High School orchestra and worked as a professional musician performing mood music on the sets of silent films.

While working on movie sets, young Russ hooked up with the glamorous Polish actress Pola Negri. The former lover of Charlie Chaplin and Rudolph Valentino, Negri no doubt showed Russ the ins and outs of Hollywood, as his career suddenly took some lucky breaks. Playing the ballroom circuit around Los Angeles, he ended up in Gus Arnheim's Coconut Grove Orchestra, which was the house band at the Ambassador Hotel.

Arnheim's band was big time in Los Angeles in the 1920s and 1930s, with many of his band members, like Bing Crosby, Fred MacMurray, and arranger Jimmie Grier, going on to achieve fame of their own. Although Columbo played violin in the orchestra, he also sang, sometimes with Crosby, whom he eventually replaced in the band.

By 1928, Columbo was performing in small singing roles in movies, often dubbing the singing for the top-billed star. The next two years were filled with cameo singing parts in quickie movies. Columbo also ran the unsuccessful Pyramid Café nightclub on Hollywood Boulevard.

In 1931, popular songwriter Con Conrad heard Columbo singing and talked him into going to New York City with him. While on the cross-country train, Conrad and Columbo wrote Columbo's signature song, "You Call It Madness." Conrad who had written the hit songs "Ma, He's Making Eyes at Me" and "Lonesome," and had also won the very first Academy Award for Best Original Song with "The Continental," from the film *The Gay Divorcee*, but at this stage of his career he focused on Broadway shows and radio.

Conrad got Columbo a radio slot on Tuesday night at 11:30 P.M. on NBC, and the young singer was soon making $3,000 a week. Conrad got the show's time changed to go up against Bing Crosby's radio show on CBS, and a fake rivalry was concocted, dubbed The Battle of the Baritones. Columbo's live performances were consistently sold out. Considered a crooner by the public, a label that Columbo hated, he was on the cutting edge of music at the time, along with Crosby and Rudy Vallee. The amplified microphone was a brand-new invention at the time and it changed the way singers sang. No longer did vocalists have to belt out songs so the people in the balcony could hear. The microphone made it possible for baritones to be heard clearly for the first time by a large audience, and Columbo took advantage of the new technology. During this time, when he was known as the Romeo of Radio and The Valentino of Song, Columbo was romantically linked with beauty queen/actress Dorothy Dell, singer/comedian Hannah Williams, and the great Greta Garbo.

In 1933, Columbo's radio program lost its main sponsor, Listerine, and the program was cancelled. After some disputes with Conrad, Columbo fired his manager, put together a band, and toured his way back to California.

Arriving in Los Angeles, he moved his family into an ornate Spanish style home at 1940 Outpost Circle in the Hollywood Hills, an exclusive neighborhood to this day.

Columbo continued to write songs and perform. Always striving to improve his talents and to help distinguish himself from all the other crooners, Columbo began taking voice lessons. He had a decent role in the film *Broadway thru a Keyhole* and sang several songs in the film.

Offered the lead role in Universal's *Wake Up and Dream*, Columbo had finally gotten top billing. With music by Cole Porter, *Wake Up and Dream* was a flop on Broadway, but was brought to film anyway. Columbo's acting had grown and his singing voice was never better. It looked like the twenty-six-year-old crooner had locked into a bright future.

On August 31, 1934, Columbo and his movie-star pal Carole Lombard attended a Friday night preview of *Wake Up and Dream* at the Pantages Theater on Hollywood Boulevard. Anxious to see the audience reaction to his first movie in which he had received top billing, Lombard and Colombo supposedly attended the festivities in disguise.

Columbo's good friend, portrait photographer Lansing Brown, Jr., also attended the preview, but Columbo didn't get a chance to talk with him after the film. Columbo wanted to know what Brown thought of his acting and the film in general. Columbo tried to reach him the next day but was unsuccessful, so Columbo drove to Santa Barbara for another preview of *Wake Up and Dream*. Lombard was exhausted from her nonstop work schedule and drove with her secretary to Lake Arrowhead for some rest and relaxation in the country. She planned on having dinner with Columbo on Sunday evening.

On Sunday morning, September 2, 1934, Columbo finally got in touch with Brown, who invited him to his home at 584 N. Lillian Way in Hancock Park. While they were discussing the weekend's events in Brown's den, Brown took one of his Civil War era flintlock dueling pistols off his desk. He was in the habit of lighting matches off the hammer of the gun, but unknown to anyone, the pistol still had decades-old gunpowder and a mini ball in the barrel. The gunpowder ignited and fired the bullet out of the barrel with such force that it ricocheted off a mahogany desk and into Columbo's left eye.

Columbo screamed as he fell into a chair. The room was filled with gun smoke when Brown's parents, who were visiting him, ran into the room. Thinking that Columbo was dead, they called the police, who found that Columbo still had a pulse. He was taken by ambulance first to Hollywood Receiving Hospital, then transferred to the Hospital of the Good Samaritan, which was better equipped for treating this type of injury. Surgery failed to save Columbo and he died in the hospital at 7:30 that evening with actress and old flame Sally Blane, film star Loretta Young's older sister, at his bedside.

An investigation cleared Brown of any wrongdoing, although there were suspicions that the two men had recently been at odds with each other. Brown took the death of his friend very hard and, according to his friends, he was never the same man. He moved out of his house where the death happened and remained a broken man for the rest of his life.

Three thousand people attended Columbo's funeral at Hollywood's Blessed Sacrament Church. Pallbearers included Columbo's friendly rival Bing Crosby, director Walter Lang, and actors Gilbert Roland and Zeppo Marx. Lansing Brown was seen in the back of the church, kneeling and crying.

Columbo's mother, suffering from blindness, was never told about her son's death. The family made excuses for the absence of her beloved son for the last ten years of her life.

CHAPTER 9

The Colossal Liar

Oakland
December 7, 1938

Airline employee Stanley Jones and his mother-in-law ventured out into the foothills above 106th Street near the Oakland Zoo early in the morning of December 7, 1938, to pick mushrooms. Thinking they had seen an animal lying in a shallow ditch, they looked closer to discover that it was actually the lifeless body of a half-naked young woman wearing a fur jacket. A deep knife wound in her chest appeared to be the cause of death, although she had several smaller wounds in her neck. Police discovered tire tracks and evidence that the body had been dragged fifteen feet to where she was unceremoniously dumped. The area was known as a local lovers lane.

The police quickly discovered that the dead girl was nineteen-year-old beauty school instructor Leona Vhught. The six-foot-tall blonde was a graduate of Fremont High School where she was an honor student. Her many female friends lined up to tell the detectives that Leona had made an early morning date with a local rogue named Rodney J. Greig.

Twenty-one-year-old Rodney Greig was a petty criminal who had his first contact with the police when he was ten years old. The handsome Berkeley resident was a thorn in the sides of his law-abiding parents. He was just no good.

Besides episodes of petty theft in the East Bay area, Greig had once done time at the infamous Preston School of Industry in Ione for breaking into his place of employment, a San Francisco wholesale grocer, and stealing two hundred and thirty dollars. He was promptly caught and arrested, yelling threats as he was being led away.

Life at the old Preston School of Industry, also known as the Castle because of the towering, red sandstone Romanesque Revival-style building high on a hill in Amador County that couldn't be mistaken for anything else, was tough, but fair. The reformatory was reserved for young offenders who were not incorrigible. The inmates were schooled and taught marketable skills to set them on a straight and narrow path toward a better life.

Some of the graduates of the Castle went on to great success, like comedian Eddie Anderson, who played Rochester on the long-running Jack Benny radio and television programs, country musician Merle Haggard, actors Rory

Oakland was a booming city in 1938. *California State Library*

Calhoun and Eddie Bunker, boxers Don Jordan and Eddie Machen, authors Neal Cassady, Phil Thatcher, Ernest Booth, and Bill Sands, casino owner Tony Cornero, and tennis great Pancho Gonzales. However, many other inmates, like Greig, went on to a life of crime or an early death.

Greig was found by police in his Berkeley home, sleeping soundly. He agreed to go with the police to the station house for questioning and quickly admitted in those pre-Miranda Rights days that he had indeed murdered the young lady, claiming that it was an accident. The police found Vhught's watch, locket, and keys in his room. They found a bloody hunting knife, along with photographs of naked women, in a back cushion of his car.

At the police station, Greig nonchalantly told the detectives that he had killed Vhught and that he threw her purse and gloves in a garbage can at 19th and Alice Streets. A little later, Greig changed his story and said that Vhught was despondent over her height and the lack of available men that were willing to date a female as tall as she was. He claimed that she was always talking about suicide.

Confidently, Greig told the police that after listening to her talk about suicide, he pulled out a large hunting knife, held it to her chest, and accidentally stabbed her. He pulled the knife out of her breast and lit a cigarette while the beautiful girl's life drained out of her. Greig smoked several more cigarettes before he decided to check to see if Vhught was still alive. Instead of feeling for a pulse, Greig took out a smaller knife and made three cuts in her neck to see if she would bleed. He told the police that he was innocent by reason of insanity. Greig waived his right to a jury trial at his sanity hearing and agreed to a bench trial presided by the Honorable Edward J. Tyrrell.

The impeccably dressed Greig slumped his head onto his chest as his insanity defense immediately wilted when one by one, six female friends of Leona Vhught debunked Greig's accusations of Vhught being suicidal. They also told of warning Leona not to go out with Greig, and that she had told them that Greig had gotten a little too fresh with her on their previous date.

Greig's former employer, from whom he had stolen money in a burglary, told the judge that outside of the theft, Greig was a good employee and as normal as any average guy.

A gas station attendant who was working the graveyard shift when he bumped into Greig in the station's restroom testified that he and Greig had exchanged pleasantries while he was washing up at the sink. Greig had been heading home from the scene of his crime at around 5:30 in the morning and seemed to not have a care in the world.

Greig's ballroom dance instructor, Rae Baker, went before the bench and said that Greig was an excellent student and seemed to be a normal, nice person. It was the only time that Greig raised his head during the testimony.

Edgar Hinkle, the owner of the boy's camp by the Russian River where Greig spent the summer of 1936, and Jack Tooley, a classmate and fellow camper, both claimed that Greig was a regular guy who never acted unusual.

Seven witnesses said that they had never seen Greig do anything abnormal. Aside from committing petty crimes and exhibiting acts of belligerence, Greig seemed to be of above-average intelligence. It was also noted that he was an excellent typist.

A parade of doctors and family members claimed that Greig suffered from epileptic seizures possibly brought on as a result of an automobile accident a few year earlier. Throughout the hearing, Greig was aloof, wisecracking with the press during recesses, but he broke down on the stand when he was being questioned and sobbed hysterically.

The prosecutors called Greig a colossal liar and were able to prove that Greig was standing outside of his car when he stabbed Vhught in the chest. They also proved that Vhught was sitting upright in Greig's car when Greig plunged his knife into her up to the hilt.

Since Greig had waived a jury trial, admitted his guilt, and gone before the judge only on a sanity issue, it was up to Tyrrell to determine the sentence. On March 13, 1939, Judge Tyrrell declared that Rodney Greig was sane. Greig showed no emotion as the judge spoke. His attorneys responded by asking for a two-day continuance, which was granted.

Two days later, on March 15, Judge Tyrrell sentenced the dapper murderer to death by the gas chamber at San Quentin Prison. It was only the second death sentence that Judge Tyrrell ever handed down. Observers claimed that Greig didn't bat an eyelash when he heard the verdict. After he was returned to the Oakland jail, he enthusiastically played a card game with fellow prisoners.

On November 9, 1939, the Supreme Court of California denied Greig's appeal and Greig went to his death on August 23, 1940. In a last act of defiance, the twenty-two-year-old Rodney Greig ripped his blindfold off as he was being led into the gas chamber.

CHAPTER 10

The Duchess

San Francisco and Sacramento
April 7 and 13, 1940

Juanita Spinelli's entire life was a lie, but she had the talent to influence the young and dumb to do her bidding. We know that Ethel Leta Juanita Spinelli was born on October 17, 1889, in Kentucky, but after that the rest of her pathetic life is speculation. Spinelli made so many claims about her past that only the truly gullible would believe a word that she said. Whether she gave herself the nickname "The Duchess," or whether it was coined by her alleged Purple Gang connections, nobody will ever know, nor probably care.

What is known about her is that she materialized in San Francisco sometime in the late 1930s, with three kids and a hood named Michael Simone in tow. Spinelli was a haggard, toothless woman who looked twenty years older than the fifty years that she claimed to be. She asserted that she was an informer for Detroit's ultra-violent Purple Gang and had to leave the Motor City in a hurry. The Purple Gang was a Jewish organized-crime outfit that was basically wiped out by internal disputes by 1935, so Spinelli's story is questionable. She was supposedly married to bank robber Anthony Spinelli, who had been killed while smuggling contraband across the Mexican border. Information on Anthony Spinelli and his crimes are as non-existent as were the Duchess' parenting skills.

The Duchess rounded up a handful of malcontents with serious mental deficiencies: eighteen-year-old Robert Sherrod, twenty-one-year-old car thief and jailbird Gordon Hawkins, and Albert Ives, a twenty-four-year-old, one-eyed half-wit. Together with the thirty-two-year old Simone, who acted as a caseman as well as the Duchess' lover, the gang knocked off gas stations and rolled drunks.

Spinelli's teenage daughter Lorraine was used as a sex lure by her criminally demented mother. Lorraine, whose street name was Gypsy, would approach drunken men with the promise of easy sex. Once they were alone, Spinelli's thugs would rob the man, sometimes taking his clothes.

Juanita thought of herself as the brains of the outfit and when she wasn't planning small-time robberies, she was cooking and cleaning for her troupe of young crooks. Acting as the teacher, Spinelli instructed the boys in the fine arts of robbery, assault, and car theft. She taught them that it was smarter to commit a steady stream of small crimes than one big one like robbing a bank. She explained that the police would go all out to find a bank robber, but they would more than likely shrug at a man who woke up on the sidewalk with his wallet missing. Providing them with the mother figure that they may never have had, Spinelli delegated jobs for the gang and doled out their cut of the money as if it were an allowance.

On a foggy night on April 8, 1940, Ives shot barbecue stand owner Leland S. Cash while attempting to rob him of the day's receipts. The fifty-five-year-old Cash was deaf and didn't hear Ives when he demanded the money. Cash reached into his pocket to turn up his hearing aid, but the dim-witted Ives blasted the restaurateur before he had a chance to comply, leaving him to die in the parking lot of his diner at Lincoln Way and La Playa in San Francisco's Sunset District.

The Duchess panicked, packed up her gang and headed for Sacramento in a stolen car, stopping only to rob a gas station on the way out of San Francisco. Settling at a cheap hotel on the seedy side of town, the gang drank whiskey and planned to make quick money by rolling drunks in Sacramento.

Much to the gang's dismay, the dim-witted Sherrod kept reliving the murder of Cash, asking the Duchess and others if they thought that Cash had died right away or if he had suffered a lingering death. The hooligans sent Sherrod out on an errand to discuss the situation.

They decided that Sherrod must die before he talked too much. Ives suggested that they shoot him in the head and make it look like an accident, but the Duchess vetoed Ives' idea. She didn't want the boy to suffer. Knowing that Sherrod was a weak swimmer, they decided to have a picnic along the Sacramento River. After the cookout, they would go swimming in the river, where they would push Sherrod into the middle of the swift spring current and to his death.

The next day, the inept gangsters piled into their stolen car and drove to an area about ten miles south of Sacramento near the Freeport Bridge with the intent to drown the hapless teenager, but Sherrod was afraid of the fast-moving current and refused to get into the water. The gang drove back to Sacramento with Sherrod blabbing on about Cash's murder.

Fearful that Sherrod would go to the police, Simone and Spinelli decided on a better half-baked plan. They put the plan into action the very next evening, April 13, 1940.

After the two younger children were put to bed, the Duchess had a get-together in her hotel room. Sherrod was anxious for a drink and downed his first glass of whiskey in one gulp. When he asked for another drink, Spinelli poured him one laced with chloral hydrate, popularly called knock-out drops, or a Mickey Finn. Sherrod gulped down the drink and was soon groggy. After he became unconscious, the gang beat the teenager, before Hawkins and Ives loaded him into the car and drove him back to the Freeport Bridge.

As Hawkins drove, Ives undressed Sherrod and put him into swimming trunks. At the bridge, Ives dragged Sherrod out of the car and tossed him over the rail into the ice-cold water. Ives placed Sherrod's clothing nearby, so it would look as if he had gone swimming. Little did Ives, Hawkins, Simone and Spinelli know, but Sherrod was already dead by overdose from the chloral hydrate.

The next day, the Duchess decided that the gang should drive to Reno. They needed to be in a fresh town full of money and drunks. They planned to rob hitchhikers and motorists along the way. The real plan was to kill the simple-minded, yet violent, Ives before he, too, started running off at the mouth. Ives was getting full of himself, bragging about the two murders that he had committed. The plan was to kill him in the High Sierras and dump his body off a tall cliff where he would never be found or even looked for.

Sometime during the ride, Ives saw Simone give Hawkins a knowing glance. At a gas station near Grass Valley, he overheard the gang talking about a 700-foot cliff. Ives wasn't as stupid as everyone thought, and he ran into a nearby diner, through the kitchen, out the backdoor and into the brush behind the diner. He waited until the gang drove away, and then he ran to a nearby California Highway Patrol post, where he told the stunned officers his story about the crime gang.

The Duchess and her crew were pulled over by highway patrol officers in Truckee. Spinelli tried to pull her innocent-mother routine, but after the police found their cache of weapons, the jig was up.

After being taken to Sacramento to face charges of Robert Sherrod's murder, the gang quickly turned on each other. Ives turned state's evidence first and told the authorities about every robbery and car theft and the two murders that the gang had committed.

Idiot criminals Gordon Hawkins and Albert Ives dumped their partner in crime, Robert Sherrod, off the Freeport Bridge and into the snag-filled Sacramento River on the orders of their crime boss, The Duchess. *Sacramento Archives and Museum Collection Center (SAMCC)*

Gypsy, who was pregnant, claimed that she had been busy attending Continuation High School in San Francisco and was too busy with school to know about the criminal deeds that her mother was involved in. She was released from custody. Eight-year-old Vincent and fifteen-year-old Joseph Spinelli were placed in foster care.

The city of San Francisco waived its right to the prisoners, and the gang was tried for the Sacramento County murder of Robert Sherrod. Gordon Hawkins, Michael Simone, and Juanita Spinelli were sentenced to death in San Quentin's gas chamber.

After the usual appeals and stunts, Ethel Leta Juanita Spinelli was led into the gas chamber on November 21, 1941. Spinelli didn't mind when the warden realized that the witnesses weren't all assembled and made her wait a few minutes while the spectators found their seats. Spinelli was the first female put to death in California's gas chamber.

One week later, on November 28, Simone and Hawkins were gassed simultaneously in San Quentin's double-seat gas chamber. Ives was found not guilty by reason of insanity and was sent to live out his life at the Napa State Asylum for the Insane.

CHAPTER 11

The Lady Killer

San Mateo/Palo Alto
1935 and 1942

For Californians, the Japanese attack at Pearl Harbor on December 7, 1941, was unquestionably a day that lived in infamy. So extraordinarily affected were the lives of Californians that the state was never the same again. Peaceful rural communities became rowdy cities overnight after massive Army and Air Force training, maintenance, and armory bases were built nearby. Idyllic seaside villages were transformed into Coast Guard and Navy ports and fuel depots. Farms in the San Joaquin and Sacramento valleys went into full production at the same time when most able men had enlisted or been drafted into the armed forces. The Bracero Program allowed thousands of Mexican citizens to come to America to work legally as manual laborers on the farms. The Mexican workers reinforced the strong Hispanic culture that has always been central to California, and suddenly English-speaking ranchers and farmers found themselves using the wrong language.

Cities experienced more hustle and bustle as thousands of men and women arrived in California, either as members of the military or to work in the industries that were being geared into a full-blown war machine. Shipyards in Long

Beach, San Diego, and the San Francisco Bay area operated non-stop on either building ships or repairing war-damaged ones. Aircraft factories in Southern California pumped out thousands of bombers, fighters, and transport aircraft. The railroads were busy carrying tanks, jeeps, and equipment from the rest of the country to the ports of California. The ports of California were in a constant state of expansion and production.

Catering to the needs of the workers, restaurants, movie theaters, drug stores, and night spots stayed open around the clock. An eat, drink, and be merry attitude arose throughout California as hundred of thousands moved to the Golden State, often without previously knowing a single soul in the state. Millions of soldiers, sailors, Marines, and airmen stopped in California for training. They all took advantage of the California good life and celebrated before they were shipped out to war in the Pacific. For many military men, the San Francisco Bay's Golden Gate would be the last sight they would ever see in America.

Thirty-year-old blond-haired beauty Bernice Curtis was one of the thousands of women who went west during World War II. Recently divorced, Curtis moved from the Chicago area to San Francisco, where her married sister lived. She shared an apartment with Elsa Martin in the Mission District and worked as a clerk at a cigar store, where she came into contact with hundreds of people each day.

On the morning of November 23, 1942, Santa Clara sheriff's deputies discovered the battered, fully clothed body of Bernice Curtis. Her fingers and jaw were broken, the back of her skull cracked, and her face shoved into the mud of the newly plowed field near the intersection of Alma Street and Diss Road, south of Palo Alto. Bernice had put up a struggle with her attacker and fought to her nightmarish death. Robbery was not the motive, as Bernice's expensive rings were left on her shattered fingers.

The sheriff's detectives re-created a scenario from the clues scattered about the crime scene. Bernice was attacked inside a green sedan and fought her way out of the car. Running down Diss Road, she tripped and fell, breaking her jaw in two places. Fearing for her life, the bloody and battered woman got up and climbed over a fence and ran into the freshly plowed field, where she was caught by her attacker, who shoved her face into the mud and then beat her head in with a nearby rock or clod of dirt. Diss Road is now known as East Meadow Drive, and is in a heavily populated suburban area, but in 1942 the area was farmland and nobody heard Bernice's terrified cries for help.

The police checked out Bernice Curtis' background and it came back clean. She had moved to San Francisco just a few months earlier to be near her pregnant sister and to start a new life after her divorce. Her ex-husband was in the Army and stationed in the South Pacific. She was well liked by her co-workers and customers, but Curtis' brother-in-law, Bernard Ash, told police that Bernice had been dating a tall, dark, and handsome Latin man named Frank.

More information was gathered concerning the mysterious boyfriend. According to roommate Elsa Martin, Bernice had been going steady with Frank for about three weeks. He was a charming man who bought a corsage of lavender, sweet peas, and gardenias for Bernice every Sunday. Bernice's sister, Helen Ash, told the police that Frank worked at a shipyard in South San Francisco, was divorced, and had a daughter. Frank had a pencil mustache and drove a green Chevrolet. A hatcheck girl who worked at the Hawaiian Garden nightclub in San Jose saw Bernice's photo in the newspaper and told the police that she had seen Curtis on Sunday night with a man whom she knew as Frank. They were with another couple, who were never identified.

The suspect was soon identified as twenty-nine-year-old Florencio Frank Alcalde, an American of Philippine ancestry

from the South Bay city of San Bruno. After the florist identified him as the man who bought Miss Curtis a corsage every
Sunday, he was arrested at Western Pipe and Steel Company,
where he worked as a shipfitter's helper. Boxes from the florist shop were found in Curtis' apartment.

Alcalde denied even knowing Bernice Curtis, but Santa Clara County Sheriff William Emig knew better. He had
dealt with Alcalde back in 1935 when Alcalde was the main
suspect in the death of twenty-six-year-old Kathleen Robinson of San Mateo. Robinson, a pretty, single woman who
worked at a laundry and gave financial help to her parents,
was found with a bullet behind her right ear on January 26,
1935. Sprawled under the Southern Pacific Railroad overpass
on East Poplar Avenue in San Mateo, Robinson was at first
thought to be the victim of a drive-by shooting.

The police put their clues together and brought Alcalde
in for questioning, where he remained undaunted by the in-
terrogation. When shown Robinson's body, Alcalde broke
down and wept.

Alcalde was released but was arrested again after the police discovered that the gun used to kill Robinson was of a
German make and so rare that there were only six of them
registered in California. One of the owners was Alcalde's father, Frank, Sr., who had reported the gun stolen two months
earlier from his San Mateo tavern.

Alcalde hired hot-shot attorney Joseph Bullock, who
pulled no punches to get his client off the hook. An alibi was
provided for Alcalde's whereabouts and he was released. San
Mateo sheriff's officers again arrested Alcalde when a search
of his room turned up an ammunition clip made especially
for the missing pistol. Again Bullock convinced the district
attorney to dismiss the case due to insufficient evidence. The
case lingered for seven long years without any new clues.

In the meantime, Frank Alcalde married and had a
daughter, but the marriage was rocky because of Alcalde's

philandering lifestyle. He had left his wife and child and moved into a South San Francisco hotel during the two weeks that he was dating Bernice Curtis. Police found bloody clothing in his hotel room and at his home in San Bruno.

At Alcalde's trial in San Jose, Joseph Bullock again represented the aloof Latin lover, but the evidence was more compelling than it had been in 1935. A green feather found at the crime scene matched perfectly a feather stub of a hat owned by Alcalde, as well as a broken inside light dome cover from a 1933 green Chevrolet sedan that was found on Diss Road near where the murder took place. Blood matching the slain woman was found on the floor mats of the green Chevrolet.

A bus driver reported that he had seen a coat that belonged to Curtis lying on Diss Road close to a parked green Chevrolet sedan with the right front door open in the early morning hours of January 25. The testimony of Curtis' roommate, sister, brother-in-law, and the florist identified Alcalde as Bernice's boyfriend. The hat-check girl from the Hawaiian Garden put Alcalde in Santa Clara County with Bernice Curtis on that Sunday evening, November 22. A south San Francisco police officer told the court that he had caught the couple necking at a lovers' lane, just a few weeks before the murder.

Alcalde's co-workers at Western Pipe and Steel, John Lopez, Leonard Scott, George Manices, and Ben Pop Moore testified that not only had Alcalde shown them photos of Curtis, but he had bragged about their sex life in vivid detail. Alcalde had told them days before the murder that he wanted to go back to his wife but that Bernice Curtis was the marrying kind, adding that he would have to get rid of her.

Lopez and Moore put the nail in Alcalde's coffin when they told the court that Frank Alcalde, Sr., had offered them money to be the younger Frank's alibi. All they needed to do was to say that they had been playing cards with the two

Alcaldes at a San Bruno pool hall. They coldly turned down Alcalde's offer and reported the conversation to Santa Clara County Prosecutor Amiglio Andrencetti.

The courtroom hushed when Alcalde's wife, Della, walked into the courtroom during a recess, grabbed Bullock without even looking at her husband, and led him into an antechamber. Moments later, she walked out of the courtroom, without once glancing at her spouse.

Frank Alcalde took the stand in his defense and denied killing Bernice Curtis. He claimed that she told him that she had a date with another man the day that she died. Nobody believed him and Andrencetti tore his alibi to shreds. The trial lasted fifteen days.

On March 10, 1943, the jury of four men and eight women found Alcalde guilty of first degree murder after deliberating for only eight hours. He was sentenced to death on March 19, 1943, but the suave and confident lady killer shrugged off the conviction, saying that he was innocent and that he would get a new trial.

The new trial never came. Alcalde's wife Della died of an illness that she caught from earning a living, leaving his young daughter an orphan on August 18, 1944, when an emaciated and ashen Florencio Frank Alcalde cursed as he entered San Quentin's gas chamber. Alcalde was the 256th person to be legally executed in California and the 42nd to die in the gas chamber.

CHAPTER 12

Head and Hands

Temple City, Los Angeles County
December 30, 1945

The Second World War abruptly changed the social fabric of America. The majority of men were off to war, leaving their wives to fend for themselves. Many women went to work in the factories and shipyards, filling jobs that were once performed by men. They became empowered by the knowledge that they could do men's work, run their households, and raise their children without the help of their husbands.

Another great change that occurred in America during World War II was that the population became increasingly mobile. Millions of servicemen from all over the country were traveling, many for the first times in their lives, to parts of the country and the world that they had never even thought about before. With its perfect flying weather, wide-open spaces, and miles of coastline, California became a logical choice for new military installations. Sleepy, whistle-stop burgs became military boomtowns, complete with all the vices of a big city.

Millions of civilians also traveled to the Golden State in search of jobs. This influx of different cultures, races, and religions opened the eyes of many who had never been exposed to people who were different from them. Small towns in isolated places were chosen to be military bases, and overnight their populations exploded, with young men and women gripped by the anxiety produced not only by the uncertainty of war but by a level of multicultural integration never before seen in these parts of the country.

Fifty-two-year-old Arthur L. Eggers was a meek, bespectacled clerk at the Temple City substation of the Los Angeles County Sheriff's Department. He was also the son of Frederick Eggers, the sheriff of San Francisco from 1912 to 1915. The elder Eggers, who came by himself to America from Germany at age fifteen, also served on the San Francisco board of supervisors from 1901 to 1906. Arthur wasn't as ambitious as his father and settled for living a normal life in the east Los Angeles County town of Temple City with his wife Dorothy and their adopted nieces, nineteen-year-old Marie and eleven-year-old Lorraine. The Eggerses also rented out the back room of their home to forty-one-year-old Leslie Loomis.

Sometime during the war, Dorothy decided that she did not want to be sexually exclusive with her husband. The timid Arthur attempted to turn a blind eye to Dorothy's late nights at local honky-tonks and the rumors of her sexual escapades, but tension rose in the Eggers household as the couple argued frequently.

On January 2, 1946, the new year was trumpeted in with the discovery of the headless, handless torso of a middle-aged woman, wrapped in a blanket and tied with a rope. The body was found in a canyon off the Rim of the World Highway in western San Bernardino County. The corpse displayed two bullet holes and the victim had been dead for less than forty-eight hours. The only clue, besides the blanket and rope, was a solitary sandal.

Arthur Eggers went to the sheriff's department at San Bernardino to view the body. He was given the brush-off by the deputy in charge, his Los Angeles County Sheriff's Department credentials carrying no weight in San Bernardino.

Back in Temple City, he tried to call his brother-in-law, who was concerned about his missing sister. Receiving no answer, he then called his renter, Leslie Loomis, and told him that the body was not his wife, as the body's feet were as big as Garbo's.

Eggers knew all along that the body was Dorothy's. He had personally tossed her body down the canyon, in hopes that she would never be found. Panic set in as he realized that it would only be a matter of time before the police figured out the crime. He hurriedly filed a missing person report with the Los Angeles County Sheriff's Department, lying about her height in an attempt to give credence to his claim that the body wasn't hers.

A few days earlier, on December 30, 1945, Arthur Eggers had returned from his swing shift job at the sheriff's department at about one in the morning. As he was getting out of his automobile, he heard the front door of his house slam. Looking down his driveway, he saw a man scurrying out of the house and down the street. Entering through the back door, Eggers walked into a darkened house. Upstairs in the bedroom, Arthur discovered his wife standing naked in the dark.

Angry at his wife's infidelity, he grabbed a .380 semi-automatic pistol out of the dresser and started to run after his wife's lover. Dorothy stopped him, and a struggle transpired in which Arthur shot Dorothy several times. He dragged her body into the bathtub and sawed off the head and hands of his wife of eighteen years. He then wrapped the corpse in a blanket, tied it up with a rope, and threw it into the trunk of her car. Driving to the isolated and mountainous Rim of the World Highway, Eggers tossed his Dorothy into the dark canyon. He returned home, cleaned up the mess, and told his nieces and boarder that Dorothy had gone out on one of her sexual conquests, probably with a soldier.

Eggers started acting like a person who was trying to hide something. He was seen on January 3 washing out the trunk of his wife's car. The next day, Eggers sold his wife's engagement and wedding rings to a jeweler for ten dollars, using an assumed name and false address.

What did Eggers in was that he sold his wife's car to a deputy who worked with Eggers at the sheriff's substation. Before the sale was completed, the deputy saw that the registration was in Dorothy's name. Eggers told the deputy that he could get her signature and it would all work out. After failing to get his niece Marie to competently forge her aunt's signature, Eggers forged it himself and sold the car to his co-worker after he had it repainted.

Arrested on January 22 on the charge of grand theft auto in Los Angeles, Eggers submitted to a lie detector test, where he was confronted with the evidence of the murder, which included blood found in the drain of his home, blood traces on the car that he had had repainted, and proof that the blanket that served as Dorothy's funeral shroud came from his home. Eggers remained cool and collected, and he passed the test with flying colors.

Oddly, almost immediately after the test was finished, Eggers broke down and admitted to killing his wife. He drew a map that led authorities to where he had disposed of his gun and the saw that he used to cut his wife up. Whether his change of mind happened because of the pile of incriminating evidence against him or because he was threatened or slapped around didn't matter; nobody cared in those pre-Miranda days.

Eggers first claimed that he threw his wife's head and hands out the window as he drove along the Rim of the World Highway on his way to dispose of her body. He led the police on a search for Dorothy's head and hands through the brush of the desert canyons near where her body was found, but after an all-day and all-night search, nothing was found.

Eggers startled the police by turning to them and casually commenting, "Well, it's almost too horrifying to tell, but here's the truth. I burned Dorothy's head and hands in the incinerator at home."

The detectives had already sifted through the ashes of Eggers' incinerator can and found nothing. Not believing Eggers, they asked him when he burned the body parts.

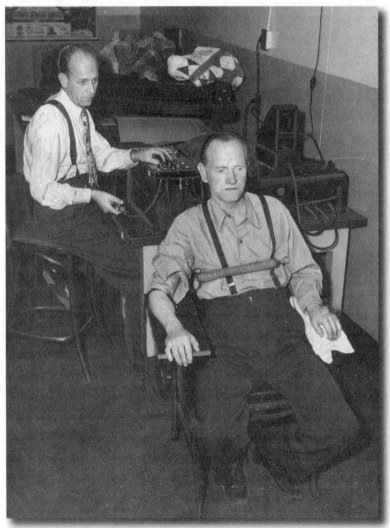

Wife killer Arthur Eggers remained cool and calm during a lie detector test. *Los Angeles Public Library*

"Why in the morning, of course," answered Eggers. "It's against the law to burn anything in our incinerator after noon."

Eggers later changed his mind about his confession, but the overwhelming evidence convicted him at his trial. There was blood in Dorothy's car trunk, in some grease on the floor of Eggers' garage, and in the bathroom in the house. The .380 bullets matched Eggers' gun, which had the worn initials AE etched onto the frame. The gun also had traces of human tissue, bone, and fatty debris. A large piece of bone fragment was found wedged between the magazine clip and the gun's frame.

Eggers became desperate and claimed that he had been framed, the jury was tainted, the body wasn't that of Dorothy, and he was insane. The judge brought in a new jury, which convicted him. He was sentenced to death, and after the inevitable appeals were denied, Eggers was put to death in San Quentin's gas chamber on October 15, 1948.

CHAPTER 13

The Deportee Plane Crash

Fresno County
January 28, 1948

Twenty-eight Mexican nationals got into an old, twin-engine DC-3 on a cold and clear Tuesday morning. The twenty-seven men and one woman were being deported back to their home country because they were working illegally in California as agricultural workers. The deportees had the choice of taking a bus, train, or airplane back to El Centro. The novelty of flying and the speed of the flight sounded much better than a long, cold, and bumpy ride.

The DC-3 was owned by Airline Transport Carriers, an air carrier that flew only flights chartered by various government agencies. The flight on that cold January day was chartered by the Immigration and Naturalization Service to fly the deportees to the INS Deportation Center in El Centro.

For reasons that remain unknown, Captain Frank Atkinson and co-pilot Marion Ewing took the wrong airplane for the flight. They were supposed to take a DC-3 that was certified to carry thirty-two passengers, but instead took a DC-3 that had seats for only twenty-six passengers and was seven hours overdue for a routine and required safety inspection. The thirty-year-old Atkinson had more than 1,700 hours of flight time and Ewing had more than 4,000 hours. Both had

Over 30,000 DC-3s were built by Douglas Aircraft Company of Long Beach, California. *California State Library*

been U.S. Army Air Corps pilots during World War II. Along with the flying crew, Atkinson's wife Bobbie flew along to serve as a flight attendant. The flight to Oakland was routine, and nothing out of the ordinary happened.

Greeted in Oakland by INS guard Frank Chaffin, the crew found out that there were more passengers than seats in the plane. It is not known if Captain Atkinson realized then that he had flown the wrong airplane or if he had been aware of the fact all along. He apparently did not care, as the plane was flying light. The flight was to travel to Burbank for refueling before heading off to El Centro. Atkinson loaded the evicted Mexicans and their guard into the plane. Three of the migrant workers had to sit on luggage. The DC-3 was slightly overloaded as it bounded down the runway and over the San Francisco Bay.

At approximately 10:30 A.M., workers at the Fresno County Industrial Road Camp, located twenty-one miles northwest of the town of Coalinga, noticed the DC-3 overhead, trailing white smoke from its port engine. Many of the one hundred men at the camp were veterans of World War II and had seen many airplanes in trouble.

Suddenly, the work crew saw the left wing ripped away from the fuselage along with nine passengers, who had jumped out through the gaping hole in the fuselage. The plane caught fire and spiraled to the ground, exploding in a huge ball of fire. The workmen ran to the scene to rescue any survivors, but the only thing that they could do was to put out the fires that the blazing aircraft had sprayed over the dry Los Gatos Canyon.

The fiery wreckage was spewed over a two-hundred-yard area. Bodies—some still strapped in their seats—littered the terrain, along with suitcases and shoes. The wing, together with the bodies of the nine jumpers, was found a half mile from the crash site. The majority of the dead were found in the front of the aircraft's burnt-out hull.

The investigation by the Civil Aeronautics Authority found that a fuel leak in the port engine fuel pump ignited a fire and, due to the extremely fast-moving in-flight air, acted like a cutting torch, burning through the wing span, causing the wing to be torn away.

The people of Fresno turned out for the mass funeral of the twenty-eight Mexican nationals at Holy Cross Cemetery. Catholic mass was said by Monsignor John Galvin of Saint John's Cathedral and Father Jose de Gaiarrgia of Our Lady of Mount Carmel. Twenty-eight identical gray caskets were laid to rest into an eighty-four-foot-long mass grave, flanked by officials from Mexico and the United States and their respective flags. Twelve of the victims were never identified.

Legendary songwriter Woody Guthrie read about the disaster at his home in New York City and became infuriated that the newspapers had omitted the names of the deportees. He wrote a poem called "Deportee (Plane Wreck at Los Gatos)" that lamented that fact. If Woody had read the *Fresno Bee*, he would have seen that everyone who was identified was named in the Fresno paper, the closest city to the accident. Ten years later, a schoolteacher named Martin Hoffman wrote music for the poem and the song was made popular by folksinger and Guthrie contemporary Pete Seeger. Over the years Billy Bragg, Dolly Parton, Joan Baez, Bruce Springsteen, Nanci Griffith, Hoyt Axton, Judy Collins, The Byrds and Peter, Paul, and Mary have recorded the song about the tragedy.

CHAPTER 14

The Snake Woman

Cypress, Orange County
July 20, 1948

Grace Olive Wiley was a pioneer in the field of herpetology, the study of reptiles and amphibians. Born in Chanute, Kansas, in 1883, she attended the University of Kansas at a time when few women went to college. She received a degree in entomology, the study of insects, but after a failed marriage, she switched her interest to the study of reptiles.

Reptiles are not the most lovable creatures. Their scaly, multicolored skin and impassive eyes set them apart from other animals. Folk tales throughout history have portrayed reptiles as sly and evil, using hypnotism to lure their prey to their deaths. The Torah, the Bible and the Koran all include the story of Adam and Eve, in which a snake entices Eve, the first female, to eat the forbidden fruit in the Garden of Eden, thus messing up humanity forever.

Snakes have been used as a metaphor for evil and death, even though out of more than 8,000 species of reptiles, only 250 have the ability to kill a human. Still, the sight of a reptile causes a primeval fear in humans that has little to do with reality.

Before Grace Wiley, widespread beliefs about reptiles in the scientific world held that reptiles are primordial creatures that have no emotion and cannot be trained or tamed. Grace Wiley's lifetime of work with reptiles disproved many of those beliefs.

In 1923, Wiley was named curator of the Minneapolis Public Library's now-defunct natural history museum, making her one of the first female zoo curators in the world. She got the job by offering to donate her enormous private collection, which consisted of 115 species and 330 individuals, to the zoo. Wiley already had a reputation among the zoological world as a reptile expert, as a few years earlier she was the first person to successfully breed rattlesnakes in captivity.

Wiley believed in treating her reptiles kindly, and she thought deadly snakes could be tamed. She believed that she could convey her sympathy to the reptiles. Refusing to use the hooks or other safety devices normally employed to handle poisonous snakes, Wiley would gently speak to them, even though snakes are deaf, and slowly and carefully stroke them until they became used to her and other human contact. Except for Gaboon vipers, which didn't like to be stroked, most of her poisonous snakes got used to being held and handled. Still, Wiley's unorthodox methods did not go over well with the zoo's administrators, who demanded that she stop handling the snakes.

Wiley used the attention to try to change the public's negative attitude about venomous snakes. Reporters rushed to interview her, and photographers loved taking photos of the matronly Wiley calmly knitting with a rattlesnake on her lap. She made good copy on slow news days for newspapers and magazines. Despite the publicity for the museum and the fact that Wiley was never bitten while working at the Minneapolis Public Library Natural History Museum, administrators gave her an ultimatum: Use safety equipment or leave. Wiley left, taking her reptilian friends with her to her new job at the Brookfield Zoo, located outside of Chicago.

When it opened in 1934, the Brookfield Zoo, also known as Chicago Zoological Park, was one of the first zoos to shun cages for its animals. The animals were put into natural settings with animals of other species that generally live with them in the wild as companions. Moats and walls separated the animals from the human sightseers. Before that time, zoo animals were locked into small steel cages that didn't allow any activity to keep the poor animals from going crazy. The Brookfield Zoo welcomed the farsighted herpetologist Grace Wiley during its inaugural year.

Wiley's casual attitude about safety made her tenure at the Brookfield Zoo brief. Wiley rarely closed the reptiles' cases and cages, and the press had a field day with sensational headlines about deadly snakes escaping the zoo. Acting director Robert Bean fired Wiley after the nineteenth venomous snake escaped.

Wiley packed up her reptiles and moved, along with her mother, to Long Beach, California, where she set up a roadside zoo. Her snakes appeared in the films *The Jungle Book*, *Trade Wind*, and of course, *Cobra Woman*. Wiley was always on the set when her animals were used, and she even appeared onscreen as a snake charmer in the 1940 film *Moon Over Burma*, starring Dorothy Lamour.

The zoo's collection grew as Wiley acquired more dangerous and exotic reptiles, and some of the species were the only ones found outside of their normal territories. The menagerie included sand vipers, asps, diamondback rattlesnakes, coral snakes, cottonmouths, black mambas, water moccasins, sand snakes, horned vipers, African spiny tailed snakes, and Dabbs and monitor lizards. Wiley carried around deadly Indian, king, Siamese and Egyptian cobras like they were kittens. Even her mother, eighty-seven-year-old Molly Gough, handled the deadly snakes. Along with giant tortoises, crocodiles and alligators, the zoo also housed a Komodo dragon, which had only been discovered by zoologists two decades before.

As a testament to Wiley's taming techniques, she was able to pet her pair of king cobras, named King and Queen. The king cobra is the world's longest venomous snake and can grow up to eighteen feet. The massive snake eats other snakes and will not eat anything that it does not want to eat. Although there is no description of the feat, Wiley had to force-feed them to keep her cobras alive. A king cobra's venom can kill an Asian elephant in three hours if it is bit on the trunk. Wiley first used a small stick with some cloth on the end to gently pet the snakes from a safe distance. Eventually King and Queen allowed her to pet the back of their heads and rarely extended their famous hoods.

This is a good example of what kindness can do for mankind, she told a reporter. What a powerful thing it must be, when even the world's most deadly reptiles respond to kindness.

Her roadside reptile exhibit charged twenty-five cents, and for that small sum Wiley would personally take the visitors through the property, even allowing children to handle the rattlesnakes, Gila monsters and cobras. Complaints from neighbors forced her to move twice, and she eventually transported the entire exhibit across the Los Angeles County line to the town of Cypress, in snake-friendly Orange County.

Although Wiley's interactions with the poisonous creatures seemed careless, she rarely let down her guard when she handled them. She had been bitten many times and she lost two fingers to her Komodo dragon's jaws, but she always blamed herself when the animals attacked her.

Wiley was named a Fellow of the Herpetologist League, the highest award given by the society. She regularly published scientific papers concerning her assessments of various reptiles, and she could pick up a rattlesnake as if it were a pet. Instead of getting a watchdog, Wiley trained her alligators to come when she called them and let them and various species of crocodiles and tortoises have free range of her compound.

Renowned freelance journalist Daniel Mannix was at Grace Wiley's reptile zoo on July 20, 1948, to finish an interview and take some photos. Wiley took off her eyeglasses for the photo session. While posing with one of her recently arrived Indian cobras, she was bitten on her middle finger while she was trying to get it to open its hood. Cobras have short fangs and have to chew to get their venom into their victim. The snake chewed on the sixty-four-year-old, 100-pound woman's finger for thirty seconds before she was able to gently pry it off. She calmly got up, walked back to the barn, and put the snake back in its cage.

Asking Mannix to get her snakebite kit, Wiley lay down while Mannix's companion ran for the telephone. To Mannix's dismay, the emergency kit was at least twenty years old. The syringes were corroded and the antidote serums' bottles were either broken or the serum had evaporated. Even the rubber tourniquet had rotted.

Wiley lapsed into a coma shortly after she was put into the ambulance and she died sixty-five minutes later in Long Beach Municipal Hospital. The hospital could do nothing to help her as it only had anti-venom serum for North American snakes.

At the time of her death, Grace Wiley wanted to retire and was in informal negotiations to sell her massive reptile collection to the Griffith Park Zoo. Her estate tried to find a buyer for the entire collection, but a buyer could not be found. The exotic animals were auctioned off piecemeal to the highest bidders. Her lifetime of work was worth only three thousand dollars. The Indian cobra that ended Wiley's life was bought by a man who displayed it as the Lady-Killing Cobra at a tourist spot in Arizona.

CHAPTER 15

The Little Girl in the Well

San Marino, Los Angeles County
April 8, 1949

Three-year-old Kathy Fiscus was all dressed up in a pretty pink dress with white embroidery on the front. She wore brand-new white shoes with pink socks. The occasion was a visit from her aunt and five-year-old cousin. The children, who included Kathy's nine-year-old sister Barbara, were playing in a vacant lot about a block away from the Fiscus home when Kathy disappeared into the ground. Barbara ran to her home and alerted her parents, who came running.

At first they could only hear muffled crying, until they discovered a fourteen-inch-wide abandoned well pipe. The frantic parents spoke to Kathy, who could faintly answer questions between sobs, as emergency and media crews arrived.

The fire department and police were unequipped for a rescue like this. They needed heavy machinery and men trained in hard-rock mining. Construction workers and experienced miners volunteered their services to save the little girl.

The rescuers estimated that Kathy was at least fifty feet down the 784-foot-deep well. A rubber ball with a wire attached was dropped into the opening and its descent stopped at 87 feet. Power shovels and digging equipment were brought in, along with volunteers who had experience in hard-rock mining and drilling. They all rolled up their sleeves and started on what would become a marathon lifesaving mission.

When the rubber ball was dropped again, it sank to one hundred feet. Kathy had slid farther down the well. Trenches were carefully dug on both sides of the well, so as not to disturb the ancient metal-encased pipe. It would take a lot of time to dig through the dirt, rock, mud, and water. Speed was of the essence, and each of the rescuers dug as if his own daughter was in the well.

Portable remote radio broadcast trucks arrived to broadcast the event to listeners all over the country. The Los Angeles television station KTLA sent a remote broadcasting unit to the scene in what turned out to be a watershed mark for the then-new medium. People throughout the entire nation sat fretfully by their radios, listening to the event unfold, and thousands of people flocked to the scene and had to be held back by police barricades.

High-powered floodlights were brought in so the work could continue throughout the night. Three large cranes helped speed the digging. Inside the freshly dug chasm, rescue workers fought solid rock, cave-ins and seeping water. Exhausted men were brought up for fresh air, but after a few breaths, demanded to be brought back down into the pit.

Well-meaning people, including people of short stature, tried to volunteer their services. Jockeys, little people from a nearby circus, and children wanted to be tied by the feet and dropped headfirst into the well to grab the little girl, but it was determined that the well casing was so badly corroded that the piping would have cut the rescuers to shreds.

The well had originally been dug in 1903 and had been used until 1932, when the corroded metal casing broke due to shifting soil and went dry. Nobody covered the fourteen-inch-wide pipe, and it sat gaping in a vacant field for seventeen years.

Ironically, Kathy's father, David Fiscus, worked as a resident manager of the California Water and Telephone Company, the company that had drilled the well forty-six years before. Even more poignantly, earlier that week David Fiscus had spoken to a group of elected officials about the need for a state law to force the capping of abandoned wells by property owners. Now David and his wife Alice bit their fingernails while waiting to learn the fate of their young child. Family and friends formed a protective ring around the couple to keep away the curious.

To fight cave-ins, the rescuers shored up the pits with aluminum sheeting, and pumps were brought in to get rid of the water collecting in the bottom of the rescue pits. The workers dug a lateral tunnel towards the well and cut a hole into the metal casing at the fifty-seven-foot mark, but only

Television was in its infancy when three-year-old Kathy Fiscus fell into an abandoned well. *California State Library*

found Kathy's pink dress. She had slipped out of her garment as she plunged deeper into the abyss.

Saturday passed without a rescue, as an estimated crowd of 5,000 people milled around the excavation. Local traffic was snarled by the sightseers, making it difficult for additional rescue equipment to get to the site. Little Kathy's anguished parents shuffled between their home and the rescue site throughout the ordeal, while cameras filmed the entire tragedy.

The next day was an unusually warm Palm Sunday, but there was no rest for the rescuers, regardless of their religious beliefs. The work went on all day Sunday, until 8:52 P.M., when Fiscus family friend Dr. Paul Hanson addressed the crowd through a loudspeaker.

"Kathy is dead and has apparently been dead since she was last heard speaking on Friday," he announced. "Her family has been notified and now we are notifying you."

The crowd evaporated as work began on bringing up Kathy's battered body. It took an hour. Kathy Fiscus had drowned in about four feet of water, eighty-five feet down the crusty old pipe. A heavy equipment operator ploughed into the old well pipe, folding it over so it could never swallow anyone again.

Later in 1949, country musician Jimmy Osbourne, who had a hit earlier that year with "My Heart Echoes," recorded the million-selling song "The Death of Little Kathy Fiscus." The song climbed to number seven on Billboard's music chart and Osbourne gave half of the royalties to Kathy Fiscus' memorial fund. Osbourne blew his brains out on December 26, 1958, despondent over his marriage and faltering career.

The vacant lot where little Kathy Fiscus fell to her death is now the football field for San Marino High School.

CHAPTER 16

Jumped the Gun

Santa Barbara

July 7, 1950

Guy Gilpatric was a successful and multitalented man who appeared to have the golden touch with every occupation that he ventured into. During his vast and varied career, he was a pioneer and record-setting pilot, setting an altitude record in 1912 at the age of sixteen after only having had his pilot's license for three months. Before the United States' entry into World War I, Gilpatric ran a flying school in Los Angeles, where he performed many stunt flying scenes for the burgeoning motion picture industry. During the war, he served in the United Stated Army Air Service as a fighter pilot in France and mustered out as a captain.

After the war, Gilpatric worked in public relations and advertising with the Federal Advertising Agency in his hometown of New York City, eventually becoming vice-president of the firm. He married his wife, Louise, in 1925, and the couple lived in the French Riviera.

As an expatriate living in France, Gilpatric created a series of short stories about Colin Glencannon, a whiskey-drinking, scuffle-attracting chief engineer of a rusty English tramp steamer. Published in the *Saturday Evening Post*, the Glencannon stories were extremely popular in the 1930s and 1940s.

Gilpatric became a prolific writer; besides the Glencannon series, he wrote semi-autobiographical stories about life in New York City at the turn of the twentieth century, flying, and living the easy life on the French Riviera. He also wrote *The Complete Goggler*, the first inclusive guide to goggle fishing.

The childless couple moved to Southern California in the late 1930s, eventually settling in Santa Barbara. In 1943, Gilpatric was nominated for an Academy Award for Best Screenplay for the Humphrey Bogart film *Action in the North Atlantic*.

On July 7, 1950, Louise became hysterical when she was told by her physician that she had a nonmalignant tumor in her breast. Allegedly, the doctor tried to explain to the panic-stricken woman that the tumor was non-cancerous; however, in a meeting with Guy, the doctor informed him that the tumor was indeed cancerous and that fifty-two-year-old Louise needed to have surgery the next day.

A few hours after the doctor's prognosis, deeply despondent over facing life without each other, the fifty-four-year-old Guy shot Louise with a .32 caliber pistol and then shot himself in the bedroom of their Santa Barbara mansion. A friend who lived in an apartment in their home found the couple the next day.

It has been widely written that the doctor had pulled the wrong medical chart and that Louise was actually cancer-free and healthy. Certainly there is some confusion about whether or not Louise had cancer, as the doctor reported that he had told Louise that the tumor was benign. It is not known if the same physician told Guy that the cancer was malignant, but there was obviously a big mistake made and the Gilpatrics fatally jumped to the conclusion that Louise did have cancer. An operation had been scheduled for 2:30 P.M. the next day, so it would appear that some kind of mix-up happened. As usual in Southern California, the case was closed as a murder/suicide and there was no further investigation.

CHAPTER 17

Penny for Her Thoughts?

Daly City
February 1, 1959

Twenty-year-old gardener August Norry had no idea what was in store for him when he was dumping yard waste in the San Bruno Mountains, just south of San Francisco, on the breezy and warm Sunday of February 1, 1959. Norry, a Korean War veteran who had been wounded in action, had taken his G. I. Bill money and gone to school to study landscape architecture. He worked full-time as a landscaper at the Lake Merced Country Club and took care of the grounds at a chemical plant in San Leandro on Sundays. Married only eighteen months and with a baby on the way, the handsome Norry was trying to make as much money as possible to support his family. Unfortunately for Norry, there isn't enough money in the world to stop determined killers from carrying out their actions.

Norry's bullet-ridden and bloody car was found at the end of a lover's lane on Christmas Tree Hill about 10:00 P.M. that night. A young boy told police that he had seen a young, blond-haired woman driving the car recklessly around 4:30 P.M. The police found Norry's bullet-ridden body in the San Bruno Hills the next day.

Forensic evidence showed that Norry had been shot while sitting in the driver's seat of his car. Blood on the inside of the door proved that the car's door was open when he was shot. He was then shot more times through the passenger side window. The car was then driven fifty yards off the road, through a barbed wire fence, to a place where Norry was unceremoniously dumped, face up on the ground, and where he was again shot multiple times. In all, there were eighteen bullet holes in Norry; fourteen of them had passed completely through his body. He had been shot three times in the head, three times in the neck, three times in the chest, twice in the stomach, and the rest were in his limbs.

Police were stunned by the overkill. They immediately believed that it was a crime of passion, given the sighting of the blond-haired woman driving Norry's car. They had made up their minds before the body was hauled away.

Norry's twenty-year-old wife, Darlene, was mercilessly questioned by Daly City and San Mateo County police, and the home that she shared with August was crudely searched. Norry's co-workers at the Lake Merced Country Club told the police that they were pretty sure that he had a relationship with a person other than his wife. Norry was a charming and handsome man. Before he enlisted in the Army, he had been a minor-league baseball player and an Arthur Murray dance instructor. Norry's family and his in-laws were at a loss as to why anyone would want to murder August. No matter how much the detectives probed, they could not find any proof of the Norrys having marital problems.

Besides the boy who saw the car drive wildly by, the only other clues that the police had obtained were a cheap blood-spattered rhinestone necklace and the unusual bullets used for the murder. They were .38 caliber blunt-nosed wad-cutters, mostly used for target practice, which were popular with firearm enthusiasts who reload their own bullets.

The police were stumbling into dead ends with the investigation. A man reported that he had seen a young, blond-haired woman with a bulldog walking toward Norry about 11:00 A.M. on the day of the murder. This and every other lead went nowhere. The police detectives hassled Norry's relatives, friends, and co-workers, hoping to find a clue, but the only thing that they determined was that August Norry was an average, friendly, hard-working family man with few close friends. Norry's brother was even a San Francisco police officer.

Two and a half months went by as San Mateo County Sheriff's Department detectives Milt Minehan and William Ridenour traced the manufacture of the bullet mold to a New Jersey company, which had sold 10,000, and then they narrowed purchases of the mold down to Bay Area buyers. One by one, Minehan and Ridenour checked out each owner, often taking samples of the gun enthusiast's bullet lead to analyze and compare with the bullets taken from the crime scene.

Eventually, inspectors Minehan and Ridenour questioned twenty-three-year-old Daly City mechanic Lawrence Schultze about his reloading practices. After taking samples of Schultze's bullet lead and comparing it against the Norry bullets, they came up with a match.

On April 14, 1959, Minehan and Ridenour confronted Schultze with the evidence; he confessed that he had indeed made the bullets and loaded them into a live cartridge. Then Schultze went further. He told the detectives that he had sold a box of fifty wad-cutter bullets to his eighteen-year-old blond-haired friend, Rosemarie Penny Bjorkland of Daly City.

Schultze also told the detectives that he had personally traveled with Penny, along with his girlfriend, who was Penny's best friend, to test-fire the rounds at San Bruno Mountain, near where Norry had been murdered.

The next day, the police were waiting at the Bjorkland home, located just three south blocks of the San Francisco city limits, for Penny to come home from work. The police were surprised by the normal working-class family with whom the murderer lived. Penny's parents and her three brothers had no idea what the police wanted with Penny.

Detectives Minehan and Ridenour were stunned when they greeted Penny as she arrived home from work. Penny was an attractive, full-figured, freckled-faced woman of eighteen. She wore her strawberry-blonde hair in a pony tail and wore ruby-red lipstick that offset her blue eyes. She wasn't surprised that the police were at her home and she gave them permission to search her room, where the detectives found newspaper clippings of the Norry murder.

Bjorkland was taken to the San Mateo County Sheriff's Department where for hours she remained tight-lipped while being questioned. Nobody knows, in those pre-Miranda Rights days, what the police did to coerce her, but Penny confessed to the murder at 5:40 in the morning. A few hours later Penny was driven to the scene of the crime.

The newspapers reported that Bjorkland had giggled while acting out her crime for the assembled police and journalists. It is more likely that the fashionably dressed, gum-chewing teenager was just being a nervous teenager, but the story was a newspaper goldmine and the media ran with it. The story had everything: a sexually charged, gum-chewing, knife-carrying, pony-tailed, freckle-faced, blond-haired teenager, who could have been your daughter, sister, or niece, and who had shot almost twenty bullets into a random person without remorse, as if she were an Albert Camus character.

Penny made an emotionless, but detailed, confession. In it, she stated that she had had the overwhelming, almost sexual urge to kill someone for several years.

"I felt better mentally," said Bjorkland. "Like it was a great burden lifted off of me. I have no bad memories about it. I always wanted to see if I could do something like this and not have it bother me."

The police were completely dumbfounded by Bjorkland. She appeared to be a polite, honest, and completely normal girl. Her existentialist attitude was something that they had never experienced in a person so young. Penny quickly expressed that she wanted to plead guilty, before she even had an attorney, but District Attorney Keith C. Sorenson wouldn't allow it.

Bjorkland impassively and rationally related to the police, courts, and the press that she had stolen the revolver from a boyfriend's parents' home in December with plans to use it to murder someone. She explained to the police that she had met Norry once before when she was on a walk on the Crocker Estate. Norry was emptying yard waste along the road and they had struck up a conversation. They went to a drive-in burger restaurant in nearby San Francisco for lunch. She didn't know that Norry was married until she read it in the newspapers, but that didn't matter because Bjorkland had no romantic interest in Norry and her only repentance about the crime was that she felt bad for Mrs. Norry.

Bjorkland had bumped into Norry by chance on the day that she killed him. According to her testimony, Bjorkland was walking on the mountain when Norry drove by and offered her a ride. While riding in Norry's car, she fired a wild shot out the window into the woods.

Once they stopped, they talked casually for a few minutes until Penny pulled out the gun and shot Norry several times. She got out of the car, opened the driver's door, and shot Norry until the gun clicked on empty. Bjorkland reloaded the gun, shoved Norry onto the passenger side and drove the car off the road, through a wire fence. Pulling Norry's lifeless body out of the car and onto the sun-baked scrub brush that dots the hills, she emptied the revolver into the unmoving father-to-be. Reloading the six-shot revolver, Bjorkland again fired six more bullets into the very dead body of August Norry.

"Suddenly," explained Bjorkland, "I had the overpowering urge to shoot him. I kept shooting, emptying my gun and reloading. That was the only reason. There was no other."

She drove away in Norry's car, ditched it, and went home to have dinner with her family. The next day, Bjorkland dumped the pistol and unused bullets down a storm drain at the corner of Camellia and Castle Manor in San Francisco.

Penny Bjorkland told her story and stuck to it.

Bjorkland described herself as a normal, average girl, but her co-workers described her as a knife-carrying lone wolf who ate her lunch by herself at her job at Periodical Publishers Service Bureau in San Francisco.

Bjorkland wouldn't talk to mental health specialists or a priest. She never cried or showed any emotion while incarcerated or in front of the judge. She told police matron Maxine Stooksbury that she hated her parents because they made her go to church.

Bjorkland's parents scrambled to find an attorney to represent their daughter. They were willing to mortgage their home to pay for legal fees. When Penny learned of her parents' anguish, she replied coldly, "They had nothing to do with it. I guess this does affect them, but that's not my concern."

Joseph Murray, the attorney hired by the heartbroken Bjorkland family, was dumbfounded by Penny's detached demeanor and unwillingness to change her story to help herself. Murray tried the usual juristic tricks to save his client, but Penny would have nothing to do with them, or with him. A dozen psychologists, including experts in experimental fields of psychology from Bay Area universities, were called in by both sides and generally agreed that there appeared to be nothing psychologically wrong with Penny Bjorkland.

On July 20, 1959, Rosemarie Penny Bjorkland pled guilty to second degree murder and threw herself on the mercy of the court. South San Francisco Municipal Judge Charles

Becker sentenced Penny to life in prison, but made her eligible for parole in seven years.

Darlene Norry gave birth to daughter Cynthia on September 17, 1958. The widow was so upset with the intrusive visits from the police that she had gone to stay with an aunt in Santa Rosa to finish out her pregnancy. She didn't know about Bjorkland's arrest until she was informed by a relative and was stunned that she and her family were still being relentlessly and rudely interrogated by various law enforcement agencies when they were already onto Bjorkland.

"They were around to insult me just before they caught her," exclaimed a rightfully angry Darlene Norry. "That is the reason I had to get away for a while."

There is no record of when Penny Bjorkland was released from the California State Prison for Women at Corona, but it is believed that she was paroled in the mid 1960s. Cynthia Norry would have been in grade school by then and never knew her father.

CHAPTER 18
Paradise Lost

Stateline, Nevada
March 1, 1964

The passengers who boarded the airplane in Salinas were in a jolly mood. After paying only $15.75 for their tickets, employees of Monte Marte, a Salinas-based goods store, and their spouses were going on a Paradise Airlines Fun Flight to Tahoe City, Nevada, to do a little gambling or take in a show. Located just across the street from California, Stateline, Nevada, is a jungle of neon-lit casinos, fine restaurants, and skyscraping hotels.

The eighteen passengers aboard the Lockheed L-049 Constellation were joined by sixty-three more passengers in San Jose, filling the four-engine plane to capacity. While on the ground, Captain Henry Norris received a weather report from the Tahoe Valley Airport. The Paradise Airlines station manager in Tahoe told the forty-five-year-old pilot that thin, broken clouds dotted the Tahoe skies. Fifteen people were bumped from the flight in San Jose, due to overbooking. One man barged through the line and demanded to be let onto the flight. He was obliged. Little did those fifteen people realize that they were the luckiest people in California that day.

Unknown to the happy travelers, Oakland-based Paradise Airlines had a less-than-stellar attitude about the safety of its aircraft. The two-year-old airline was a scheduled, intrastate California carrier, flying four leased airliners between Oakland, San Jose, and Lake Tahoe. The airline had no maintenance crews or facilities of its own, outsourcing such work to an FAA-approved maintenance station in Oakland. The Civil Aeronautics Board later found out that the mechanic who worked on the Constellation's compass had never worked on that model before and did not take the time to check with any technical manuals for help. A different mechanic adjusted the altimeters, and he later told CAB investigators that he could not recall if he had tightened a vital screw.

Taking off at 10:30 A.M. for the approximately one-hour flight, Captain Norris flew his packed airliner east over the Sierra Nevada Mountains and into a blinding snowstorm. According to the CAB, Paradise's Tahoe station manager, apparently reluctant to turn away a lucrative flight, had changed an official weather report, notifying Captain Norris in San Jose that Tahoe was only partially cloudy, when, in fact, there was a raging snowstorm and icy conditions.

At 11:21 A.M., Captain Norris reported to the Federal Aviation Agency in Oakland that he had sighted the south shore of Lake Tahoe and was going off instruments for a visual approach to the Tahoe Valley Airport. Not expecting the severe weather and flying one of the oldest models of the four-engine passenger liner, which did not have de-icing capacity, Captain Norris radioed Tahoe Valley Airport for a weather report. Visibility at the airport was zero. Norris radioed that he was at 15,000 feet and gave his position as over Meeks Bay on the west shore of Lake Tahoe, approximately fifteen miles from the airport. When the tower asked if he was going to divert to Reno, Norris answered, "No."

At 11:29 A.M., Norris radioed the airport, "Flight 901" and then there was silence. The stunned control tower crew frantically tried to contact the plane, but to no avail. After not receiving any response from Flight 901, they could only hope that Norris had taken his plane over the mountains for a safe landing in Reno. At the time, the airliner had only three hours of fuel left in its tanks.

A multiagency search for Flight 901 began that afternoon, coordinated between California's Placer and El Dorado counties and Douglas County, Nevada, and led by Captain Bruce Cummings of the Western Air Rescue Center based at Hamilton Field Air Force Base in San Rafael. The search groups spread out over the vast, mountainous area. Cabin cruisers went out onto Lake Tahoe to search for any sign of debris or an oil slick. Sheriff's deputies quizzed mountain residents to determine if they had heard a plane or an explosion. In the meantime, the storm kept dumping snow in the area. The odds that Flight 901 had not crashed were only a little better than winning the slots in Stateline.

The next day, an air force helicopter took off from Stead Air Force Base near Reno to begin an air search for Flight 901. Lake Tahoe was teeming with white-capped waves and clouds rimmed the snowy Sierra Nevada peaks. Captain

Paradise Airlines Flight 901 crashed in these snowy mountains just a few miles from the California state line, and 85 Californians lost their lives. *Sacramento Archives and Museum Collection Center (SAMCC)*

Leroy W. Marx discovered the crash site on Genoa Peak, at an approximate altitude of 8,500 feet. The scene was so severe that it was hard to distinguish between the wreckage, stumps, and boulders. On the next pass, the pattern of the debris emerged in such a way that it looked like an unfinished jigsaw puzzle, with many parts missing. An engine was still smoldering. The distinctive three-rudder tail of the Constellation was the largest piece of wreckage.

Several feet of new snow covered the wreckage that had been strewn nearly 1,000 yards as the plane first sheared off the tops of trees and then crashed into a clearing. The fuselage was in a cluster of trees about 200 feet from the tail of the aircraft. The passengers in the fuselage were mostly all burned, while the passengers in the tail section were relatively intact. Clothing and body parts littered the landscape. There was evidence that some of the passengers, perhaps ones who weren't wearing their seat belts, were punched through the ceiling of the plane, leaving body-shaped holes in the roof. Had the aircraft been flying a mere 300 feet higher or 1,000 feet farther south, it would have safely cleared the crest of Genoa Peak.

The Civil Aeronautics Board investigations later determined that the Constellation's altimeter had malfunctioned at least eleven times in the prior eight months. The day before the crash, a different pilot who was flying the plane had reported that his altimeter had been sticky, remaining motionless during descents, then suddenly registering a 150 to 200 foot drop. The copilot's altimeter had registered 100 feet below sea level when the plane was on the ground at the Oakland airport. The crew also reported major errors with the aircraft's compass system, often off as much as fifteen degrees. Three days after the crash, Paradise Airlines' operating license was suspended, and when the airline's license expired, the Civil Aeronautics Board refused to renew it.

CHAPTER 19

Suicide Via Airliner

San Ramon, Contra Costa County
May 7, 1964

G ordon Rasmussen had just finished milking the cows on the farm where he worked in eastern Contra Costa County when he heard the engines of an airplane sputter overhead, followed by a loud explosion. On a nearby hill just off Tassajara Road, a black cloud of smoke rose into the air and a herd of cattle were seen stampeding back toward the ranch.

The crash shook the quiet country life from all the near-by residences. As ranchers, workmen, and volunteer firemen raced to the scene, they could tell that there would be no sur-vivors. The Fairchild F-27 Turboprop had almost vaporized upon impact with the hillside. So little was left of the wreck-age that the fire went out by itself due to lack of flammable material. There wasn't enough of the airplane left to burn.

The Pacific Air Lines Flight 773 had taken off earlier from Reno at 5:54 A.M., with thirty-three passengers and three crew members. It was piloted by Captain Ernest Clark, a veteran flyer whose bomber had been shot down during World War II in the Mediterranean Theater. The copilot controls were in the assured hands of thirty-one-year-old Raymond Andress, and thirty-year-old Marjorie Schafer was the sole flight attendant for the short flight to San Francisco, which included a stop in Stockton.

Flight 773 was a gamblers' special, operated in cooperation with the Reno Chamber of Commerce and Harrah's and Harold's Club casinos. The package deal included two free drinks, free limousine service to and from the airport, a free buffet dinner, and a $15 refund. The catch was that the customers could not bring any luggage and had to take one of the last three evening Pacific Air Lines flights to Reno and leave on one of the first three flights out of Reno the next morning.

In Stockton, two passengers departed and nine passengers boarded for the half-hour trip to the City by the Bay. The two lucky passengers who deplaned had no idea that they had just escaped with their lives, as Pacific Air Lines Flight 773 took off back into the air at 6:38 A.M. Less than ten minutes later, the packed airliner took a forty-five degree dive into the hills twelve miles northwest of Danville. The plunge was so sharp that the wreckage was compressed to only a two-acre piece of scorched earth.

Oakland air traffic controllers received a garbled message from Flight 773 before it disappeared from their radar. The controllers hailed a nearby United Airlines flight for a visual confirmation. The United pilot, who was flying at six thousand feet, a thousand feet higher than the Pacific Air Lines flight had been assigned to, replied that he could see a puff of black smoke rolling off the hills, but no fire.

The crash scene was a panorama of horror, with pieces of luggage, clothing and bits of human flesh littering the hillside. Hundreds of bent silver dollars, winnings from Reno slot machines, were scattered about the crash site. Firemen found a bloody, twisted, and cocked .357 Magnum revolver in the debris and turned it over to the police. It wasn't unusual for passengers to carry firearms aboard a commercial air flight in those days before hijackings and terrorism became rampant.

Among the forty-four dead were San Francisco police inspector George Lacau and his wife Betty, along with their friends, San Francisco tavern owners Paul and Georgette Marty. They had traveled to Reno to gamble and party for the night. Gospel singer Polly Johnson got on the plane in Stockton. She was on her way for the first date of a planned tour. Popular Reno radio disk jockey Rodger Brander also boarded the doomed flight in Reno. Dale Stopp lost his mother Patricia and his wife Judy. Helen Allrich of Lodi was on her way to her sister's funeral. The entire Kendricks family—Donald and Norma and their two sons, three-year-old Richard and one-year-old Douglas—were on their way to Pennsylvania to visit Norma's mother, who had never seen her grandchildren.

The F.B.I. and the Civil Aeronautics Board sifted through the rubble to find clues concerning the tragedy. The F.A.A. listened to a tape of the last garbled radio message from Flight 773. They believed that the message said, "My God, I've been shot!" The investigators looked more closely at the blood-smeared revolver.

One passenger was unaccounted for. The scribbled name on the passenger list appeared to be Mr. Beakley or Beckley. It was soon discovered that the mysterious man turned out to be the cause of the accident.

Frank Kiko Gonzales was used to living an upper middle-class lifestyle in his native Philippines. The twenty-seven-year-old Gonzales had stopped in San Francisco on his way back from competing as a yachtsman for the Philippines in the 1960 Summer Olympics in Rome. Gonzales liked San Francisco so much that he stayed, got married, and had a son. But Gonzales had to take a couple of social steps down in America. He worked as a forklift driver at a Hales department store warehouse and as a part-time waiter at the St.

Francis Yacht Club. Gonzales would sometimes work as a crewman on the yachts of the people he served food to.

In addition to working two or three jobs at a time, Gonzales had become a serial gambler and had recently been kicked out of his home by his wife of two years. Patricia had had enough of Gonzales' gambling and erratic behavior. They had a one-year-old son together and Gonzales was gambling away his paychecks before he even received them.

While living with his brother at 1278 6th Street in San Francisco, Gonzales continued his downward spiral. A man of contradictions, he was fond of children but wouldn't support his own son. He was deeply religious, but swore like a Marine. He was outgoing, articulate, and affable, but was a debt-ridden, compulsive gambler with a serious depression problem. He would disappear for days at a time without telling anyone where he had been. On May 6, Kiko took a Pacific Air Lines gambling flight to Reno for one last shot at winning big. Gonzales bought $100,000 worth of flight insurance before he left the Reno airport for the casinos. He was now worth more dead than alive.

The F.B.I. was able to trace the gun to a man in Reno. He told police that he sold the gun to Gonzales for $130 on the day before the crash and that Gonzales had paid with an insufficient funds check. Further investigation confirmed that Gonzales had shown the gun to several acquaintances in Reno and told them that he was going to die within twenty-four hours.

Gonzales lost at the tables that night, telling a dealer that it was no big deal and that he was going to die soon anyway. Frank Gonzales boarded Flight 773 with the other passengers for the flight back to San Francisco.

On November 2, 1964, the Civil Aeronautics Board ended its investigation into the crash of Flight 773. The inquiry concluded that passenger Frank Gonzales entered the cockpit after the plane left Stockton and shot the pilot and copilot, causing the plane to nosedive into the hills twenty-one miles southeast of Oakland. All six bullets in the cylinder of the large handgun had been fired. Whether others were shot is unknown, as none of the found body parts were big enough to test. The final transmission from Flight 773 was analyzed by Bell Labs in New Jersey. The message, audible after some electronic tweaking, left no doubt about what had transpired: "Skipper's shot! We've been shot! I was trying to help!"

CHAPTER 20
Bobby Fuller

Hollywood
July 18, 1966

Born in Baytown, Texas, on October 22, 1942, and raised in El Paso, Bobby Fuller entered his teenage years at the same time that rock-'n'-roll became a sensation. Fuller and his younger brother Randy formed their own rock band, the Embers, which later changed its name to the Fanatics, and eventually became known as the Bobby Fuller Four. After playing bars, dances, and clubs throughout southwest Texas, Bobby Fuller opened a teen dance club, the Rendezvous, in El Paso. Building their own home-recording studio, complete with a jerry-rigged echo chamber, the Fuller brothers released records on local labels Yucca and Todd Records, and on their own label. Fuller also recorded and produced local rock bands at his studio.

In 1964, the Fuller brothers closed the Rendezvous and moved to Los Angeles in search of fame and fortune. With his tapes under his arm, the handsome Texan had no trouble getting gigs in Hollywood, including a residency at PJ's, where the band broke attendance records.

Signing with Bob Keane, who had discovered Ritchie Valens and Dick Dale, and also owned a number of record labels including Donna, Del-Fi, Mustang, and Bronco Records,

Fuller started releasing singles under various names. The Bobby Fuller Four appeared in the movie *Ghost In The Invisible Bikini* and were wooed by the legendary producer Phil Spector, who sat in on piano on some of their live shows. Local hit songs "Let Her Dance" and "Never To Be Forgotten" failed to chart nationally, but the ambitious Fuller plowed on, appearing on televised teen dance shows *Shindig*, *Shebang*, and *Hollywood A Go-Go*.

In October 1965, Fuller recorded "I Fought the Law," a song written by former Cricket Sonny Curtis. With its ramped up guitars and outlaw lyrics, it was just what the youth of the day wanted to hear, and the song reached the top ten on the U.S. charts and the top forty in England. As his third national single, "The Magic Touch," was released, Fuller had disagreements with Keane over the direction of his career. Fuller was a rocker and a songwriter and wanted to stay that way. Keane, on the other hand, wanted to decide what would be A-sides and nixed plans for a live album that Fuller was enthusiastic about recording. Keane also canceled the Bobby Fuller Four tour of England. Bobby dropped out of his national tour and made plans for a solo career.

In the early morning hours of July 18, 1966, Bobby received a mysterious phone call and left his apartment. It was the last time he was seen alive. About five in the afternoon, Bobby's mother found him in his car in front of his apartment building at 1776 Sycamore in Hollywood. She first thought that he was asleep, as he was wearing his pajamas, but she soon found out differently. Fuller was dead, his body beaten, and the interior of his car drenched with gasoline. The police called it a suicide, saying that Fuller doused himself with gasoline inside of his car, but passed out from the fumes before he could light himself on fire.

The police neglected to mention the fact that Fuller was a successful young musician who had everything to live for and that his stomach was full of gasoline. Fuller had cuts and bruises on his chest, face, and shoulders, a hairline fracture in his right hand, and dried blood around his chin and mouth. The coroner ruled that the gasoline had been poured on his body and down his throat after he died.

Bobby Fuller had a girlfriend named Melody, who worked at PJ's as a waitress. There were rumors that she was a part-time prostitute and the girlfriend of the co-owner of PJ's, Dominic Lucci. Lucci supposedly had East Coast mafia connections. His partner, Adel Nasrallah, a.k.a. Eddie Nash, was a well-known character who over the years has escaped numerous convictions for drug trafficking, arson, and murder. It is believed by some that Lucci, jealous over Melody's affection for the good-looking and talented Fuller, had his goons work him over to teach him a lesson about dipping into the company ink. Fuller, a confident Texan, probably put up a fight and got the worse of it. In a panic, the goons tried to cover up the murder by burning up Fuller and his car, but got scared away from the scene by a passing police car.

Another theory is that Bob Keane and his partner in Del-Fi Records owed some organized crime figures money. Keane had taken out a life insurance policy on Bobby for one million dollars. When the mobsters learned of the insurance policy on Fuller, they may have killed him to make Keane pay off his debt and to teach him a lesson to pay his bills.

There is no way of knowing just how far Bobby Fuller would have gone in his music career, but chances are that the driven, good-looking musician from El Paso would have been a major force in the music industry, especially with the advent of the musician-producer in the 1970s. Unfortunately for Bobby Fuller, in the 1960s, he may have been worth more money dead than alive.

CHAPTER 21

Death House in Davis

Davis, Yolo County
April 7, 1972

In the early 1970s, Davis wasn't the sprawling community it is today, where college students and wine-drinking executives live elbow to elbow in shabby apartments and monstrous cookie-cutter homes. The Yolo County city, located twelve miles west of Sacramento, was a tranquil farming community, anchored then, as now, by the University of California, Davis, with its prestigious schools of medicine, law, agriculture, engineering, and veterinary medicine. Aside from shoplifting and stolen bicycles, the city was a relatively crime-free environment. That is, it was until April 7, 1972, when a crime occurred that shook Davis to its very foundation.

Dr. Larry Z. McFarland was the forty-one-year-old chairman of the veterinary anatomy department at University of California, Davis. McFarland had worked his way through UC Davis by toiling as a janitor, eventually earning his degrees and professorship. Dr. McFarland was renowned for his research on the connection between the now-banned pesticide DDT and its effect on the thickness of the eggshells of birds. DDT in the food chain made the shells too thin, leaving the embryonic bird susceptible to the environment.

McFarland was married to Sophia Simmons, a native of Czechoslovakia and a registered nurse. Over the years, the couple had three children—Kenneth, Michael, and Nina—and by all accounts appeared to be a happy family.

In the early 1960s, the McFarlands bought the eighty-five-year-old Frank Chiles Mansion on East 8th Street, next to the city cemetery on Pole Line Road. The family spent a decade remodeling the two-story, nine-room Victorian home and landscaping the surrounding property. They created twelve acres of park-like grounds on which their children could play in serenity with their menagerie of dogs, horses, ducks, and doves. The McFarlands decorated their home with expensive antiques and heirlooms that they carefully selected.

The doctor spoke frequently to his colleagues about his happy family activities, but all was not well at the McFarland home. The couple had separated, with Larry moving into apartment 18 at 1521 E. 8th Street, a dozen or so blocks away from the home.

Sometime during the evening of April 7, 1972, Dr. McFarland went to his family's home and bashed in the skulls of his forty-five-year-old wife and his three children. He dragged their bodies to the upstairs master bedroom and laid them side by side, face up on his bed. Nina was nine years old and Kenneth was ten. Fourteen-year-old Michael was at a school dance and was probably the last to be murdered when he arrived at home sometime after 11:00 P.M. The demented doctor then locked the doors to the mansion, splashed gasoline all over the first floor, and ignited a blaze that took firemen forty-five minutes to contain.

McFarland was found sprawled across his family with his head blown off by a double-barreled .20 gauge shotgun. A two-page letter was found in his pickup truck with detailed instructions for funeral services and numbered and itemized instructions for the disposal of the twelve-acre estate, which he had left to his mother. McFarland left no explanation as to why he murdered his entire family, other than stating that his family should remain together in life and death.

Sophia's mother, Mary Simmons, refused to allow Larry to be buried with his family and fought for the ownership of the property. Once she gained title of the estate, she never set foot on it again. The city of Davis grew up around the once-isolated property, which is now surrounded by duplexes and apartments that were built in the 1980s and 1990s. The property came to be worth a fortune, but Simmons refused to sell, leaving it as a shrine to her only child and grandchildren. Eventually, the animal sheds and outbuildings rotted and collapsed. Overgrown flower gardens choked fences that held back the happy memories that were so abruptly shattered on that cold Saturday night.

For more than thirty-six years, the Simmons property remained fallow. Mary Simmons died in 2006 at the age of ninety-eight. Having no direct descendants, Simmons left the property to six living relatives, who sold it 2007 to a real estate developer for $4.2 million.

CHAPTER 22

Death in an Ice Cream Parlor

Sacramento
September 24, 1972

The third annual Golden West Sport Aviation Air Show at Executive Airport in Sacramento was winding down. The planes that performed at the event were beginning their taxi routes to fly out. The column of airplanes was long, too long for pilot Richard Bingham, who voiced his complaint to the control tower. Bingham was piloting a Korean War-era F-86 Sabrejet, a fuel-guzzling and temperamental plane, one of the first combat jet aircraft in the United States Air Force inventory. The F-86 was a hard-edged aircraft, difficult to control at low altitudes. It routinely stalled if its nose wheel lifted off the ground when taking off at speeds slower than 140 knots.

Bingham decided to take off on a shorter and less crowded runway to save on fuel. He held an air transport pilot's license—one of the highest-qualified licenses a pilot can have—but he only had twelve hours of flight time in the F-86.

The blue and gold single-engine jet rolled down the runway, lifted its nose off the ground, bounced back down, and then lifted off. But the aircraft stalled, lost altitude, and clipped an old levee. The fuel-filled drop tanks ignited, causing a huge fireball. The F-86 bounced, landing on Freeport Boulevard, bounced again, and slid into the corner window of Farrell's Ice Cream Parlor.

Farrell's Ice Cream Parlor was one of two businesses open in the Crossroads Shopping Center that Sunday afternoon. As many as 100 people, many of them children, were enjoying a refreshing treat when the flaming F-86 slammed into the restaurant.

Twenty-three people, including twelve children, died from multiple causes. The entire Krier family—Warren and Sandra and their two children, Brandon and Jennifer, ages two and eight respectively—died in the inferno. Nine members of another family also died. Twenty-five people were injured.

When the fire department pulled the plane out of the wreckage to look for bodies, they found two automobiles melted together underneath the plane. Inside one of the cars were the bodies of an elderly couple who had been driving

Shocked fire fighters extinguish the burning jet that slammed into a Sacramento Farrell's Ice Cream Parlor, killing twenty-three people. *Sacramento Archives and Museum Collection Center (SAMCC)*

on Freeport Boulevard when the Sabrejet bounced on top of their car.

To his credit, pilot Bingham rode the plane down instead of ejecting from the out-of-control and blazing plane. He luckily survived, suffering a broken leg and arm. A passerby pulled him out of his burning aircraft.

Sacramento firemen search through the debris of Farrell's Ice Cream Parlor after a civilian-owned F-86 crashed into it on September 24, 1972. *Sacramento Archives and Museum Collection Center (SAMCC)*

Farrell's Ice Cream Parlor is long gone. The new Sacramento police headquarters is now located where the Crossroads Shopping Center once stood. On March 15, 2003, a memorial was dedicated to the victims of one of the worst on-ground air disasters in American history.

CHAPTER 23

There Goes the Neighborhood

Alameda
February 7, 1973

It was a typical winter evening in Alameda—scattered rain, partly cloudy, and chilly. The residents of the island city, located southwest of Oakland, had no idea that their evening would turn into a scene from hell.

High above the San Francisco Bay, a pair of Vought A-7E Corsair II jets were on a routine training mission. Mission leader First Lieutenant John Pianetta and his wingman, twenty-eight-year-old Lieutenant Robert Lee Ward, had taken off from Lemoore Naval Air Station at 7:30 P.M. in their single-engine, sub-sonic attack aircraft. Their flight plan was to fly to Sacramento and turn west before heading back to base after flying over the San Francisco Bay.

While flying over the eastern side of the bay at 28,000 feet, Pianetta noticed that Ward's plane had slipped away from sight. Radioing Oakland Air Traffic Control to report that he had lost his wingman, he requested and got permission to turn around and descend to 14,500 feet to try to locate the missing jet.

An anonymous naval officer stationed at nearby Alameda Naval Air Station told the *Oakland Tribune* that he heard the aircraft screeching and instinctively knew that the plane was flying too fast to be coming in for a landing at the base. Looking up, he saw the plane encased in flames. It was not a normal landing pattern, he reported. It was not any kind of a pattern.

Witnesses all over the northern part of the San Francisco Bay saw Ward's A-7E Corsair fall out of the overcast sky. Most of the eyewitnesses said that it looked like a meteor and was only visible for seconds before it exploded into a huge orange and black cloud of smoke and fire.

The blazing, ten-ton aircraft slammed into a corner of the three-story Tahoe Apartments in the middle of the city of Alameda at 8:13 P.M. White-hot flames fed by the airplane's half-filled fuel tanks tore through the twenty-seventh unit at 1814 Central Avenue, as the building collapsed due to the force of the crash and explosions. Flaming debris sprinkled the neighborhood, igniting other fires, especially in the neighboring apartment houses, which were destroyed. The explosion rocked Alameda and blew out windows for blocks.

There were many instances of terrified tenants being saved by strangers who ran through smoke and flames to rescue them. Mona McIntire was watching television in her apartment when suddenly the power went out and the building seemed to jump, knocking her to the floor. She was saved by an anonymous man who climbed up a drainpipe to the third floor and pulled her out through a window. The wounded stumbled out into the street like zombies.

Crowds of people came out into the streets to see the incredible fire, making it difficult for the police and fire department to access the scene. Blaring sirens and announcements through loudspeakers couldn't make the crowd budge. The throng seemed hypnotized by the flames and superheated air. They stood in disbelief, unable to comprehend what was happening in front of them. Finally, police fought and pushed their way through the crowd with fire trucks and ambulances following right behind them. But when the firemen hooked up their hoses to the hydrants, they found little pressure in the lines. Too many fire trucks were hooked up to the city's water system. Eventually, a U.S. Navy fire team arrived and dosed the debris with fire retardant foam used in airplane crashes. Ten firemen and three police officers were injured during the disaster.

Recovery efforts were hampered by rain, which turned the site into a quagmire of muddy ash. The authorities had no idea how many bodies would be pulled from the disaster area. Not only did they not know how many residents had been at home at the time of the disaster, they had no idea how many visitors might have been in the area.

Among the dead was Mervin Burford, his wife Dorothy, and their eighteen-month-old son, Michael. Burford had mustered out of the Navy earlier that day and was no doubt looking forward to starting a new life with his family. Navy wife Renee McComber and her infant son Kevin were also incinerated. Her husband was at sea, serving on the aircraft carrier *Hancock*. Sandra Humfreville was killed shortly after she arrived at her apartment. She had probably just hung up her coat when the Corsair crashed into the wood and stucco building.

A few days later the engine of the A-7E was found buried fifteen feet deep in the ground, telescoped and twisted to two-thirds of its original size. The ejector seat's emergency handle was found in the wreckage, meaning that Lieutenant Ward did not eject out of the plane and drown in the bay.

The death toll was eleven, including Lieutenant Ward. Forty people were injured. Eight of the victims were completely incinerated. Only a few personal effects of Lieutenant Ward were found.

Navy investigators found evidence of a cockpit fire and theorized that the line feeding oxygen to Lieutenant Ward's mask had somehow caught on fire. There was speculation that Lieutenant Ward, who was a cigarette smoker, had lit up in the plane, but Ward had served for six years as a Navy flight instructor and it was highly unlikely that the by-the-book career Naval aviator would do such an incredibly risky thing. It is more likely that if Lieutenant Ward was still alive while the plane was crashing, he was doing his best to ride the burning plane down to avoid crashing into a populated area. Unfortunately, he crashed right in the middle of an island city.

CHAPTER 24
Yuba City Loses a Generation

Martinez
May 21, 1976

If you happen to be driving south on Interstate 680 outside of Benicia you will see a wonder of geography, the Carquinez Strait, where the San Joaquin and Sacramento rivers meet and flow into San Francisco Bay. At this spot, millions of gallons of water flowing down from the mountains surrounding the Sacramento and San Joaquin valleys are funneled through the mile-wide slice in the Coastal Range, where they slam into the rising and receding salt-water tides of San Francisco Bay. During springtime, at high tide, when the tributaries of the two rivers are swollen with the runoff from the melting mountain snow, the Carquinez Strait looks like a river of cold boiling water.

In the 1930s, a railroad bridge was built over the straits. A highway bridge was erected in 1962, and in 2007, a second bridge was finished to carry the northern lanes of I-680. Before 1962, cars and trucks had to take the ferry to cross the waterway.

The year 1976 marked the bicentennial of the signing of the Declaration of Independence and the entire nation was draped in red, white, and blue and was in a festive mood. Special events and parades were planned throughout the summer, and school groups were traveling all over the country to perform. The Yuba City High School a cappella choir were no doubt enjoying the beautiful spring weather on their end-of-the-year school trip to perform at Miramonte High School in Orinda. Fifty-two people crowded into a 1950 Crown school bus owned by Herb Brown's Friendly Service Station. The Marysville business had skipped the bus' last state inspection because they were planning to sell the bus in the near future.

While being driven by fifty-year-old Evan Junior Prothero, the bus rolled onto the Benicia-Martinez Bridge and was exiting I-680 onto Marina Vista Road in Martinez, just a half hour from their destination, when Prothero lost control of the bus and crashed through the guardrail of the off-ramp. The bus flipped upside down and fell twenty-eight feet to the ground, landing on its roof, before sliding another thirty feet on its roof. The bus was crushed up to the lower window level.

Rescuers fight valiantly to save some of the fifty-two victims of the bus crash outside of Martinez in 1976. *Sacramento Archives and Museum Collection Center (SAMCC)*

Pools of blood seeped out of the bus, as the sounds of crying and the moans of the injured passengers mingled with the dust in the air. Police and ambulances rushed to the scene, along with a crane from a nearby construction site, but there

Skidmarks and missing railing chart the path of death for twenty-seven teenagers and one adult. *Sacramento Archives and Museum Collection Center (SAMCC)*

was nothing the rescuers could do for twenty-seven students and one instructor except to take them to the morgue. Twenty-four people, including the driver, were seriously injured.

When the bus was lifted up by the crane during the rescue effort, lifeless arms and legs dangled from underneath. It took hours to free the injured and remove the dead, and East Bay hospital emergency rooms were pushed to their limit.

Besides the students, chaperone Christina Estabrook was killed in the crash. Her husband, music teacher Dean Estabrook, who was driving ahead of the bus, saw the accident from his rearview mirror.

The tragedy shook Yuba City and its twin city, Marysville, across the Yuba River, to their cores, as almost everyone in the area knew someone who died in the crash. One family, the Engles, lost their twin seventeen-year-old daughters, Sharlene and Carlene. Seventeen-year-old Tom Randolph survived the accident, but his twin brother Robert perished. The severely injured Prothero was questioned by the National Transportation Board in December. Prothero attested that the brakes had failed and denied that he was driving too fast on the exit ramp. The board concluded that the accident probably was caused by faulty brakes.

For the twenty-three injured students, their families, and the families of the dead, life would never be the same. Yuba City had lost a generation.

CHAPTER 25

Anissa Jones

Oceanside, San Diego County
August 28, 1976

Anissa Jones will always be known as Buffy, the pigtailed blond girl who was eight years old for five seasons on the 1960s hit CBS television show, *Family Affair*. The show starred Brian Keith as Uncle Bill, a wealthy New York City bachelor who adopts his brother's three children after he and their mother die (how they died is forever a mystery). Distinguished British actor Sebastian Cabot played Uncle Bill's gentleman's gentleman, Mr. French. The show revolved around the resulting hilarity as the three children, teenage Sissy and twins Jody and Buffy, tried to adapt to a new lifestyle with two men they barely knew.

Family Affair was a bona fide hit, placing fourteenth in the ratings in 1966–1967, its first year on the air. In the 1967–1968 season it tied with *The Dean Martin Show* at number four. The next year *Family Affair* tied for fifth place with the long-running westerns *Gunsmoke* and *Bonanza*. During season five it came in at number five, but by the 1970–1971 season it failed to rate at all and the show was dropped by CBS.

The show was produced by Don Fedderson, who was famous around Hollywood for his torturous production schedules, usually working his non-star actors six days a week, all year long. Fedderson, who also produced another hit show for CBS, *My Three Sons*, allowed Brian Keith, as well as *My Three Sons* star Fred McMurray, an easier production schedule than he laid on his co-stars. All the scenes with Keith or McMurray were filmed in two thirty-day blocks, so the two stars could be available for film work. This schedule meant that everyone else on the program had to film their scenes out of sync with the actual show that they were working on. Any frame that Keith wasn't in was filmed later.

In her role as Buffy, Anissa Jones was a sickeningly sweet little girl who constantly carried, and talked to, a large, ugly, eyeglasses-wearing doll called Mrs. Beasley that resembled an old-fashioned schoolmarm. The doll was mass-produced and sold in the millions. So stiff was Fedderson's style that Buffy never aged in the five years that the program was broadcast. Nor did her hairstyle or clothing change—blond pigtails that stuck out of the side of her head and out-of-fashion Little Bo-Peep dresses.

As Jones matured into a teenager, Fedderson had his wardrobe people cover her breasts with bindings to make her appear to be eight years old. To add insult to injury, Jones' mother Mary, an aggressive stage mother, and Fedderson kept Anissa busy with public appearances in order to promote the various merchandise with her and Mrs. Beasley's images on them, long after Anissa hit puberty. She was forced to carry Mrs. Beasley around and act like an eight-year-old when she was thirteen.

When CBS cancelled *Family Affair* in 1971, Jones was happy that it was over. She rejected most acting roles that came her way and tried to be a normal teenager. Anissa and her younger brother Paul, who were inseparable, became pawns in their parents' divorce, until their father John was finally awarded full custody in 1973, only to die shortly afterward from a heart condition. The two teenagers were forced to moved in with their mother in Playa del Ray.

A rebellious teen, tired of working a grueling schedule under hot lights, Jones wanted to go to a regular school and hang out with people her own age. Mary arranged for Anissa to be tossed into Juvenile Detention for staying away from home for days at a time and for having failing school grades.

Anissa got a job at a Winchell's Donut Shop in Playa del Ray, something that must have deeply embarrassed her mother. Hanging out with the stoner beach crowd, Anissa started to drink alcohol and smoke marijuana, waiting patiently for her eighteenth birthday when she would get $70,000 from a trust fund and $107,800 worth of U.S. Savings Bonds. When the money came in, she and Paul didn't waste a minute leaving their mother's home and they rented a nearby apartment.

Always putting her brother first, Anissa bought him a brand-new and fully accessorized Camaro and she bought a brand-new Ford Pinto for herself. Together the siblings took the drug usage up a notch when they started snorting cocaine and angel dust and eating an assortment of downers. Alcohol and weed were always around, and their apartment quickly became known as a twenty-four-hour party house.

On August 28, 1976, just over five months after receiving her trust fund money, Anissa Jones was found dead in a friend's house in Oceanside. Clad only in boxer shorts, Jones had overdosed on a combination of quaaludes, secobarbital, cocaine, and angel dust. When her friends back in Playa del Ray learned that she had died, they broke into her apartment and stole everything of value.

It was rumored that her stomach was a mass of coagulated medication. Whatever the truth, San Diego coroner Robert Creason put it bluntly, Anissa Jones' death was one of the most severe cases of drug overdose ever seen in San Diego County. The apple-cheeked little girl who never aged in 138 episodes of *Family Affair* would forever be eight years old. Keeping with family tradition, Paul Jones died of an overdose in 1984.

CHAPTER 26

Bob "The Bear" Hite

Los Angeles
April 5, 1981

"This shit won't even get me high." Those were the last words of Bob "The Bear" Hite, lead singer of the blues/boogie band Canned Heat, best known for its entrancing single "On the Road Again." Hite was a huge, gregarious man—hence his nickname—and like most musicians during the sixties and seventies, he had a penchant for booze, drugs and wild living.

Hite was born on February 26, 1943, in Torrance, California. His father was a radio sportscaster and the family moved about the country during his elementary school years. Back in California in his teens, Hite made a deal with a guy who changed the records in jukeboxes each week to sell him all the 78-rpm records that he was taking out of rotation for one dollar. This was the start of Hite's giant record collection, which at his death was one of the biggest collections of 78-rpm blues records in the world.

After high school, Hite worked at Rancho Music, a record store in West Los Angeles, where he met guitarist Henry Vestine and guitarist/harmonica player Alan Wilson. Together they formed Canned Heat with Hite on vocals. As deeply into the blues as any of their contemporaries, like the Paul Butterfield

Blues Band, Hite piloted Canned Heat into a quintessential party band. The band's performance at Woodstock was so legendary that its rendition of the Son House song "Going Up the Country" turned into the unofficial song of the three-day festival of peace. Canned Heat also performed at the Monterey Pop Festival in 1967, as well as at hundreds of other music festivals around the world.

Hite's great achievement was producing and playing on the landmark 1970 album Hooker 'n Heat. Teaming the hippie blues band with the then fifty-three-year-old bluesman John Lee Hooker was a boon to everyone's career; sadly, it was the last project that Alan Wilson was involved in before he died of a drug overdose on September 3, 1970. Wilson was found in a sleeping bag on a hill behind Hite's Topanga Canyon home, although it appeared that persons unknown had brought him there after he had died.

After Wilson's death, Hite's personality changed. He became Bear Hite, the unstoppable, yet lovable, party animal. Fun-loving to a fault, Hite would party with fans after the shows at the slightest suggestion. He would snort the most cocaine, take the most LSD, smoke the biggest joint, eat more speed and downers, and drink more booze that anyone in whatever room he was in at the time. His appreciative admirers would give Hite massive amounts of free drugs and, like other talented artists before and after him, drugs got the best of Hite.

For eleven years Canned Heat chugged along the touring circuit, playing mostly in outlaw biker bars, especially in Australia. There were drug busts, which caused problems whenever they tried to cross an international border, and a revolving door of personnel changes on guitar and bass.

On April 5, 1981, Canned Heat was playing a show at The Palomino Club in North Hollywood. The Palomino Club was run by brothers Tommy and Billy Thomas and was the place in Los Angeles for country and blues bands to play. Over the years notable musicians such as Johnny

Cash, Patsy Cline, Buck Owens, Merle Haggard, Waylon Jennings, Lefty Frizzell, and hundreds of other like-minded musicians performed on the stage of The Palomino Club. The club was notorious for its lack of backstage security, and dozens of well-wishers were in Canned Heat's dressing room when someone offered Hite a vial of heroin. Thinking that it was cocaine, Hite stuck the vial up his nose to a collective gasp.

"This shit won't even get me high," chuckled Hite as he inhaled the vial's entire contents. Hite immediately turned as blue as a Smurf and fell, all three hundred-plus pounds of him, like a tree. Panic ensued backstage and well-meaning fans fed Hite cocaine, holding a straw to his nose, with Hite impulsively lifting his head to snort the drugs off the surface of a mirror. Two roadies tried to walk Hite around to bring him to, but to no avail. Knowing Bob's high tolerance to drugs, the roadies put him into a van and took him to the nearby home of Canned Heat's drummer, Fito de la Parra. Eventually, an ambulance was called and Bob "The Bear" Hite died of a heart attack brought on by a combination overdose of heroin and cocaine. He was thirty-six years old.

CHAPTER 27

The Keddie Murders

Keddie, Plumas County
April 11, 1981

The early 1980s was a financially difficult era for many California families, especially those in the rural northern part of the state. The Sharp family was one of the thousands of families who had to make do with less. James Sharp had taken a job out of state while his wife, Glenna, whom everyone called Sue, stayed in Cabin 28 of the Keddie Resort near the Plumas County village of Keddie, along with their sons John, Rick, and Greg, and daughters Tina and Sheila. At an elevation of 3,200 feet and surrounded by the pine-covered Sierra Nevada Mountains, Keddie is about as far out in the wilderness that you can go while still having modern conveniences.

The Keddie Resort was built in 1910 to take advantage of the new eastern rail line built by the Western Pacific Railroad. As an alternative to the steeper and higher Donner Pass route, the new route took passengers and freight over the lower Beckwourth Pass and on to Salt Lake City.

The resort became a popular place for Northern California city folks to take a vacation without traveling too far away from home. The resort once offered a large rustic lodge with rooms, a restaurant, and thirty-three cabins, as well as hiking trails and trout fishing in the nearby streams. The lodge restaurant was noted for its exotic native game menu, which featured such delicacies as barbecued bear ribs and sherry-basted raccoon steaks.

With the advent of better roads and roomier automobiles after World War II, families didn't have to travel by train to get out into the wilderness and the glory faded from the Keddie Resort. By the late 1970s, the cabins were mostly rented out to transient workers and families down on their luck—like the Sharps.

Friday, April 11, 1981, was like any other Friday night for the Sharp family and the close-knit community of Keddie. Fourteen-year-old Sheila stayed overnight at a neighboring friend's home, while a thirteen-year-old schoolmate of Rick stayed overnight with him at Cabin 28. The friend was later identified as Justin. It would be a night of watching *The Love Boat* on television and eating popcorn. Fifteen-year-old John was hanging out with his seventeen-year-old friend Dana Wingate; he, too, planned on spending the night at the Sharps' cabin.

Dana Wingate was living at a receiving home in the town of Quincy, ten miles down Highway 70/89. By all accounts, Dana was basically a good kid, but he displayed some behavior problems. He smoked marijuana and sometimes drank alcohol. In a small county like Plumas, the police officers know who you are even if you have never had a run-in with the law. Wingate had permission from the manager of the receiving home to stay overnight at the Sharps' cabin as long as he didn't hitchhike to get there.

Being typical teenagers, John and Dana ignored the only rule given to them and hitchhiked to Keddie. They first stopped at a party just off the highway at Oakland Camp. As in any rural area, there was nothing for teenagers to do except have bonfires, drink beer, smoke pot, and have sex. It must have been a quiet night at Oakland Camp because neither of the boys were seen drinking or smoking pot at the party. They left to hitchhike the rest of the way to Keddie around 10:15 P.M.

The next morning, Sheila came home to find her mother, John, and Dana lying tied up, beaten, and butchered in the living room. She ran back to get her friend, and together they found Rick, Greg, and Justin safe and sound in a back bedroom, having apparently slept through the entire slaughter. They pulled them out through the bedroom window.

The police were flabbergasted at the display of extreme violence at the crime scene. Streaks of blood were splattered over all the walls in the room. All of the victims had been tied up with electrical cord and duct tape. Their faces were beaten to a pulp, and they all had multiple stab wounds. The murder weapons lay in the open. All were simple household articles—a steak knife, a butcher knife, and a claw hammer—all covered in gore. The blade of the steak knife was bent into a U-shape, such was the rage of the attackers. Worst of all, thirteen-year-old Tina was nowhere to be found.

Cabin 28 at the Keddie Resort years after the murders. *Courtesy The Comtesse DeSpair*

Outside of the cabin, officers found evidence that the angelic, blond-haired and blue-eyed Tina had been abducted, and that she was probably seriously injured.

The news of the murders shocked Plumas County and all of California. Multiple homicides just don't happen in places where the entire county's population would fill a minor-league baseball stadium.

The oddest thing about the crime was that nobody had heard anything. Two adolescent boys and a toddler slept through the entire bloodbath. Neighbors hadn't seen any unusual activity at the Sharps' home either. Even more strange was that Cabin 28 was smack in the middle of the Keddie Resort, only a stone's throw from all of the other cabins.

Investigators from many different California police agencies and the FBI lent their expertise to the Plumas County Sheriff's Department. After 4,000 hours of investigation, they came up with the following scenario:

With the cabins so close to each other it is a mystery why nobody heard four people being murdered. *Courtesy The Comtesse DeSpair*

John Sharp and Dana Wingate hitchhiked from the party at Oakland Camp around 10:15 P.M. and were picked up by persons unknown, who tricked them into taking them home to Cabin 28. They may have asked to use the telephone or bathroom. The two teenagers were attacked simultaneously and without warning with objects found in the home. Sue, being a typical mother, became aware of the commotion and appeared in the living room, where she was murdered. She was the only victim who had defensive wounds. She was found naked with a blanket tossed over her. Her hands were tied together and her throat had been slit. The teenagers were tied together with electrical cords. John was found face-up, with bound hands and feet. The cord from his feet was connected to Dana's feet; he was face down with his head on a cushion. The teenagers had been beaten with hammers and various pieces of furniture. The steak knife had been pounded so violently into one of the victims that the blade was bent

The back entrance of Cabin 28, where Tina Sharp was dragged away by the unknown assailants. *Courtesy The Comtesse DeSpair*

180 degrees. At some time during the beatings, Tina woke up and entered the slaughter room. The police did not think that she survived the attack and for unknown reasons was taken away by the murderers.

The only evidence was one unknown fingerprint found on the back step rail post. A button was also found near the same stairs. A blood-soaked, blue windbreaker jacket, with white and red stripes, was found near Wingate's feet, and a white toolbox was missing from the kitchen. All of the blood in the gore-streaked living room was type O, the same blood type that the entire Sharp family shared. The curtains were closed, and the only light on in the house was in Sue's bedroom. The phone was off the hook.

The people of Keddie, a typical small town, pointed fingers and made accusations, but everyone who was investigated was cleared. The Sharps had lived in Keddie only since November and although they were poor, they were well-liked. Many thought that the murderers hopped off a train on the nearby railroad tracks and went to Cabin 28. As often happens when there is a senseless and brutal murder, Satan worshippers were blamed, although nobody in the area knew of any worshippers of Satan.

Plumas County Sheriff Dough Thomas asked for anyone with any information, no matter how insignificant it might seem, to come forward. He let it be known that anyone who was at the party at Oakland Camp would not be questioned about underage drinking or illegal drugs if they were interviewed by police. But nobody came forward.

In the spring of 1984, a bottle collector found the skeletal remains of Tina Sharp near Feather Falls in Butte County, over sixty miles north of Keddie. The case has never been solved and sometime in either 2002 or 2004, Cabin 28, long boarded up and feared as haunted, was torn down.

CHAPTER 28

The Caldecott Tunnel Explosion

Orinda/Oakland
April 7, 1982

O f all the engineering accomplishments that the human race has achieved, none causes a greater sense of dread and claustrophobia than a tunnel. There is nothing natural about entering a hole in a mountain or under a river, and not being able to see the light at the end of the tunnel.

The Caldecott Tunnel is a three-bore motor vehicle tunnel that carries State Highway 24 from the eastern Contra Costa County cities of Walnut Grove, Orinda, and Lafayette through the Berkeley Hills and into Oakland and Berkeley. Tunnels one and two were finished in 1937; tunnel three was added in 1964. Tunnel one handles eastbound traffic and tunnel three, the northernmost tunnel, is for westbound traffic. Tunnel two reverses direction, depending on the busiest traffic times. It usually runs west from midnight to noon and east from noon to midnight. At 3,771 feet, tunnel three is 161 feet longer than its older twin neighbor. While not exactly a lengthy tunnel, it was cut through the rugged Berkeley Hills, and the climate can be completely different from one opening of the tunnel to the other, with the hot air from the Sacramento Valley on the eastern side and the cool maritime air of the San Francisco Bay on the western portals. During the summer, it is not unusual for the temperature to vary forty degrees between the portals.

Thirty-four-year-old Janice Ferris was driving west on State Highway 24, after having drinks with friends in Walnut Grove. With a blood alcohol level of 0.17 percent, over twice the legal limit, the San Leandro bookkeeper made it one-third of the way through tunnel three when she sideswiped the tile walls while negotiating the gentle turn that occurs in the middle of the tunnel. Ferris stopped in the left-hand lane to inspect the damage to her vehicle and her car was struck by the front tire of an Armour Oil Company gasoline truck driven by Mervyn Metzker. The truck, a tanker pulling an extra tanker trailer full of the extremely flammable fuel, pulled over into the left-hand lane.

Just then, an out-of-service Alameda County Transit bus swerved into both vehicles, buckling the metal sides of both of the tankers, tipping the trailer over. The bus driver, fifty-five-year-old John Dykes, was thrown out of the bus and probably died instantly. Janice Ferris also apparently died as a result of the collision. The driverless bus then careened down the tunnel, bouncing off the walls until it smashed into a concrete pylon at the western egress.

The gashed tankers gushed 8,800 gallons of gasoline into the tunnel, which sloped uphill at a 4.7 percent grade to the west. Adding to the spectacle were numerous small fires which broke out around the wreckage. In the meantime, vehicles kept entering tunnel three, unaware of the serious accident deep inside the tunnel.

June Rutledge was returning with her son Stephen from Carson City, Nevada, in her small pickup truck, loaded with items for a garage sale she was planning. Seeing that there was a major accident in the tunnel, the fifty-eight-year-old reporter stopped the truck and ran to the emergency phones that are spaced at intervals throughout the tunnel, while her thirty-one-year-old son ran back through the tunnel warning drivers to turn around. About twenty vehicles entered the tunnel after the initial accident, but thanks to Stephen Rutledge—and the smoke and reflected flames—most were able to turn around or back out of the tunnel. Trapped in the tunnel were an elderly couple and two men in a semi-truck, which was carrying beer.

As the fires intensified, a dark, dense cloud of smoke started rolling to the eastern opening of the tunnel. Stephen Rutledge became too overwhelmed by the heat and thick smoke to go back to help his mother, and he started running out of the tunnel as fast as he could. As Rutledge and trapped fellow

The Caldecott Tunnels were finished in 1937. A third tunnel was added in 1964. *California State Library*

driver Paul Petroelje escaped from the tunnel, the small fires came together and ignited the gasoline tankers. An exploding fireball raced to the entrance of the tunnel, just like in a bad action movie. June Rutledge was on the emergency telephone when she was incinerated by the blast.

The natural west-to-east breeze that usually blew through the tunnel and the 4.7 percent uphill grade to the west virtually turned the tunnel into a horizontal chimney, with the flames exiting the western side of the tunnel. The eastern side of the tunnel remained almost untouched. This proved to be Mervyn Metzker's saving grace, as he ran east to the safety of an emergency escape tunnel.

Besides Ferris, Dykes, and Rutledge, sixty-eight-year-old married couple George and Katherine Lenz died of either smoke inhalation or the fireball that reached 1,800 degrees. Beer truck driver Everett Kidney and his passenger Edward

Young died as they stepped out of their semi-truck. In all, seven people died due to either the collision, the smoke inhalation, or the fireball.

The only thing that the Orinda and Oakland emergency crews could do was to let the fire burn itself out, which it did in less than an hour. The wreckage inside the tunnel reminded firefighters of a war zone, with melted trucks, cars, and trailers. Strangely, the semi-trailer containing the beer remained intact, with charred cans of beer hissing away their carbonated lives.

CHAPTER 29

Bill Graham

Vallejo, Sonoma County
October 25, 1991

The live entertainment industry can be divided into two eras—before and after Graham—due to the talented efforts of an orphaned Holocaust survivor named Wolfgang Grajonca, who later changed his name to Bill Graham. Grajonca was born in Berlin on January 8, 1931, to Russian Jews who immigrated to Germany to escape the turmoil in postrevolution Russia. Grajonca's father died a few days after he was born, and he wound up in an orphanage not long after. Along with his sister, he was sent to France in an exchange for Christian children, and thus he miraculously survived World War II. He was sent to an American foster home after the war. Most of his immediate family wasn't so fortunate—one of his sisters didn't survive the journey to France, while his mother and an older sister ended up in Auschwitz, where his mother died.

Wolfgang's thick German accent didn't go over well with the neighborhood kids in the postwar Bronx, and he quickly learned to speak like a local. He changed his name to Bill Graham, a name that he claimed to have picked out of a phone book. He also learned to act like a no-nonsense New Yorker, a trait that would serve him well in his business career.

After serving in the Korean War, where he was honored with the Purple Heart and Bronze Star, Graham went to work in the Catskills' hospitality business. While there, he learned valuable lessons about working with entertainers that would serve him well in the years to come.

Graham moved to San Francisco in the early 1960s, just in time for the great culture shift that would be centered there. He managed the San Francisco Mime Troupe and promoted his first concert on November 6, 1965, a benefit to cover the legal fees of the troupe after they were charged with obscenity at an outdoor engagement. The concert made an astounding amount of money and Graham—ever the capitalist—saw bigger opportunity ahead.

Graham immediately started to manage, promote, and book the swarms of psychedelic rock bands that were converging onto the San Francisco music scene. He took a lease on the Fillmore Auditorium at 1805 Geary Street and presented his first show on February 4, 1966, headlined by the Jefferson Airplane.

In short time, Bill Graham was presenting a virtual who's who of late sixties West Coast rock, as well as touring bands of the era. California bands such as Blue Cheer, Big Brother and the Holding Company, The Grateful Dead, Quick Silver Messenger Service, Love, and Country Joe and the Fish shared the bill with out-of-town groups such as Jimi Hendrix, The Who, The Doors, Pink Floyd, Cream, and the Electric Flag. Even the Velvet Underground and Nico appeared, accompanied by Andy Warhol and his Exploding Plastic Inevitable psychedelic extravaganza, one of Warhol's few outings outside of New York City. Graham, who liked to mix up his shows, would book older rockers as well as blues and jazz musicians such as Lightnin' Hopkins, James Cotton, Miles Davis, and Chuck Berry on the same bill with the young, white hippie bands, making for some of the most innovative and eccentric concert lineups in history.

Graham was fearless in both business and life. He took a lot of grief from leftist hippies who wanted his concerts to be free of charge, and Graham got into many young radicals' faces, telling them where to get off. He would go toe-to-toe against misbehaving members of the Hell Angels motorcycle club. Even though Graham had set up a security team, he would often personally throw out individuals who snuck into the venue without paying. At the same time, he hired local hippies to run his events, giving jobs to long-haired, bead-wearing young people at a time when having long hair was still an oddity. Graham gave teenaged Carlos Santana a job at the Fillmore after he caught him trying to get into his second floor office from the outside. Graham was so impressed with the future guitar legend's determination to see the show that he hired him to work at the auditorium.

In 1968, Graham's entertainment empire opened the short-lived Fillmore East, a venue in his native New York City, and he obtained exclusive booking rights to the 5,400-seat Winterland Arena and the 10,000-plus-capacity Cow Palace in San Francisco. In 1972, Graham promoted the West Coast portion of the Rolling Stones' world tour. He also managed Bob Dylan's comeback tour with The Band in 1973.

After closing his venues in the early 1970s, Graham took a long vacation in Greece. When he returned, Graham was firing on all cylinders, putting into place a grand plan that would change the way that rock concerts were presented and basically give his company, Bill Graham Presents, monopolistic rights to most rock music events on the West Coast. Putting bands in large venues like parks, sports stadiums, and arenas raised the price of tickets and added to the gross excessiveness of the drug-fueled musicians of the modern era of rock. Gone were the hippies running the door and providing security, as professional security guards were installed and different levels of backstage access were provided by laminated cards. Graham ventured into marketing the groups that he represented, selling t-shirts and posters in the venues where his shows were booked. By the 1980s, Bill Graham controlled every aspect of concert promotions, from tickets to venues. He was taking in money by the truckload.

Graham did so well that he gave up the day-to-day operation of Bill Graham Presents and concentrated on benefit concerts for the many causes in which he believed. Over the years, Graham raised millions of dollars for charity but, unfortunately, his benevolence caused his death.

On October 25, 1991, Graham wanted to personally ask the band Huey Lewis and the News to perform at a benefit for the victims of the recent Oakland firestorm that had left thousands of people from Oakland and Berkeley burned out of their homes. The group was performing at the Graham-controlled Concord Pavilion in Contra Costa County, about twenty-five miles east, as the crow flies, from Graham's Corte Madera home in Marin County.

Although there was a nasty storm hitting the San Francisco Bay area, Graham had helicopter pilot Steve Kahn take him and his girlfriend, Melissa Gold, across the bay and over to Concord to get Lewis to sign onto the benefit. After securing Lewis for the show, Graham and Gold jumped back into the Bell Jet Ranger helicopter and took off for Corte Madera. Somehow the helicopter strayed off course, flying low over the tidal marshland north of San Pablo Bay and crashing into a 200-foot-tall high-voltage electrical tower. The helicopter burst into flames on impact, killing all three aboard and making lights flicker all over the San Francisco Bay metropolitan area. The charred remains of the helicopter hung grotesquely in the power lines for more than a day.

The Concord Pavilion has changed names a half-dozen times since Bill Graham's tragic death, and ownership of Bill Graham Presents changes hands like Monopoly property, but the sign still reads, Bill Graham Presents. Not bad for a Jewish orphan who escaped the Nazis.

CHAPTER 30

Vince Welnick

Forestville, Sonoma County
June 2, 2006

Vince Welnick was a gifted pianist and singer who was as troubled as he was talented. Born in Phoenix, Arizona, on February 21, 1951, Welnick started playing keyboards during his teenage years. He eventually joined a hometown band, The Beans, which merged with the Red, White and Blues Band and became The Tubes. After the band moved to San Francisco, The Tubes became an over-the-top theatrical rock band known for the Phil Spector-ish "Don't Touch Me There," the MTV hit "Talk to Ya Later" and the ultimate stoner rock opus "White Punks On Dope." The seven-piece band of superb musicians were fronted by the chameleon vocals and outrageous stage antics of Fee Waybill and a host of props and scantily clad female dancers.

Even though The Tubes released records and toured the world, they never attained a smash hit record. Their elaborate stage shows were expensive to produce, involving a bloated payroll of roadies, dancers, seamstresses, carpenters, and sound and light technicians to feed, house, and pay while on tour. The Tubes always put on an entertaining and musically hot show, leaving all the attendees in good cheer. But the record companies that they signed with never knew what to do with the group until MTV came along. Even then, it was a little too late for The Tubes and they were once again dropped by their record company.

Welnick, his talent at the piano undeniable, stayed busy doing session work and going on tours with Todd Rundgren, Dick Dale, and the String Cheese Incident, but he found his destiny by joining the legendary rock band The Grateful Dead after keyboardist Brett Mydland overdosed in 1990 at age thirty-eight.

Welnick's melodic playing and ability to sing high harmonies fit right into the style of The Grateful Dead, and soon frontman Jerry Garcia and Welnick became friends. Although Welnick never recorded a studio album with The Grateful Dead, he toured with them until Garcia's untimely death of a heart attack while undergoing treatment for substance abuse in 1995 in Forest Knolls, Marin County.

Garcia's death devastated Welnick. He bounced around in the Mickey Hart Band, Ratdog, Jack Straw and with his own Missing Man Formation, but depression got the better of him. While on a Ratdog tour, Welnick overdosed on drugs in an apparent suicide attempt and was diagnosed with clinical depression. After the overdose, Welnick was ostracized by the surviving members of The Grateful Dead and wasn't invited to play on group-related affairs like the 1998 Other Ones and 2002 The Grateful Dead Family Reunion tours.

Welnick wasn't in the best physical health, either. Just before The Grateful Dead's last tour in 1995, he was diagnosed with throat cancer and emphysema. He beat the cancer, but his resilience was weakened by the ordeal, and made worse by his refusal to quite smoking cigarettes and marijuana.

A dejected and depressed Welnick stopped taking his medication in order to address his problems without the shield of the anti-depressant drugs. On June 2, 2006, he stepped into the backyard of his Forestville home and slit his throat. It was reported that he fought all attempts to stop the bleeding. Vince Welnick, the effortless keyboardist, died at the age of fifty-five.

CHAPTER 31
Talkin' 'bout My Generation

Laguna Beach
April 22, 2007

The results are coming in for the first generation exposed to television, and they don't look good. Raised in front of the idiot box since the day they opened their eyes, the children born in the 1950s and 1960s have ripened into a bloated and soulless bunch of materialistic and irresponsible fools. Influenced by the programs that they mindlessly stared at through puberty—where every situation gets solved in an hour—and bombarded with advertisements that brainwashed them into thinking the product was fashionable, they've turned into exactly what they criticized their parents for being, only worse.

Before the Public Broadcasting Service, or PBS, was launched in 1970, television for children consisted mainly of *The Three Stooges* and *Our Gang* comedies from the 1930s and poorly animated *Popeye* and Hanna-Barbera cartoons. PBS came out of the gate with *Sesame Street* and *Mr. Rogers' Neighborhood*, programs that actually taught the young masses something and culturally connected them for life, but it was too late for the children who had been raised on television before that. Television journalist and author Tom Brokaw called the generation that grew up during the Great

Depression and fought in World War II The Greatest Generation. Sadly, their children may go down in history as The Substandard Generation, a generation that believed in a world where anyone can become rich or grow famous without having to put any effort into the endeavor. Because they think that once something is achieved, everyone lives happily ever after, The Substandard Generation has doomed itself to disappointment.

Kevin and Joni Park were part of that generation. The Mission Viejo parents of three probably saw those late-night commercials in which you too could become a millionaire.

Kevin had worked for the U.S. Postal Service until an injury in the early 1990s put him on disability. The Parks had been married since 1984 and lived in a modest home in Mission Viejo in Orange County, but according to family and neighbors, Joni felt that the large, master-planned community with the lowest crime rate in the county was beneath her. Joni was preoccupied with class status and became the neighborhood paranoid crank, calling the police about neighbors who parked in front of their home and for other inane incidents. She would snap at neighbors because she didn't like their choice in roof tiles and fences. Kevin did his best to smooth things over, but it wasn't easy, as Kevin had an aggressive personality. Joni's habit of berating wait staff and store clerks didn't make her any more endearing.

The couple ran a small real estate investment company and they apparently hedged their investments against an expected inheritance from Kevin's father, Oliver Park, who owned investment property in California and Hawaii. When Oliver died on March 29, 2007, at the age of eighty-two, Kevin and especially Joni expected Oliver's property holdings to be worth millions of dollars.

Kevin and his older brother Patrick, a retired grocery store manager from Placentia, were named executors of the estate. A third brother, Michael, had died in 2001. The will instructed the brothers to divide large chunks of property equally, while a smaller percentage was to go to Michael's three children. On April 19, the brothers spent two hours going over their father's accounts and paperwork at a Bank of America branch. They discovered there was no fortune to inherit.

Joni, who was fond of parading around her home in the nude, hit the ceiling when Kevin told her the news. The heavy-set woman's paranoia got the best of her and she went into a panic, believing that her brother-in-law, nephew, and nieces were trying to swindle them out of money that didn't exist.

The next day, Joni called the police to report what she thought was happening to them. She told the officer that her in-laws were out to kill them for the money. The officer took a report and left.

Calling her twenty-three-year-old daughter Christie at her San Francisco Bay Area home, she demanded that she fly home immediately for a family meeting. Christie, a UC Berkeley college graduate who worked for a marketing firm, obeyed her mother and caught a flight to San Diego.

On the evening of Saturday, April 21, Joni Park checked into the luxurious Montage Resort and Spa in nearby Laguna Beach. She checked in under an assumed name and paid cash for a $2,200-a-night bungalow. Later that evening, Kevin, Christie, seventeen-year-old K.C. and eight-year-old Amanda Park arrived at the resort carrying at least seven boxes of financial documents, a printer, and the entire contents of their safe. They also brought along a semi-automatic pistol.

The family ordered room service and discussed the financial situation. Things seemed to be better when Christie went to bed around two in the morning. When Christie awoke around seven, she found that her parents seemed like they were scared, nervous. When Joni started waving the pistol around and acting irrational, Christie grabbed her little sister and left the bungalow. K.C. left shortly afterward.

The Laguna Beach Police Department started to receive multiple calls around 7:30 in the morning about a naked, crazy woman running around the grounds of the Montage Resort. She was carrying a gun and was pointing it wildly at guests and employees.

Joni was back in her bungalow (and dressed) by the time the police arrived. A few minutes earlier, Kevin and K.C. had disarmed the distraught woman who, when she wasn't walking around naked, was fond of wearing flowered muumuus.

K.C. was outside talking to the officers when Joni pointed the gun through the sliding glass door of their suite at the cops in a threatening manner. Kevin then took the gun and pointed it at the officers. The police, believing that there was a real possibility that either one of the two might shoot at them, fired on Joni when she took the gun and pointed it at them. When she was knocked down by the bullets, Kevin picked up the gun and immediately was shot by the police officers. Although wounded, Joni picked up the pistol one more time before she was mowed down by the police. Kevin and Joni each had been hit by four bullets, and they were very dead. Joni's zeal for money and status had caused the deaths of two people and left two minor children orphaned.

The *Los Angeles Times* interviewed anonymous relatives who said that the couple had acted odd for years. Another added that he found it strangely poetic that, after bragging about their inheritance for so long, it became their undoing. Michael Park's widow, Caroline Park, put it more bluntly. "There's not one tear shed for her," she told a reporter from the *Los Angeles Times*. "Not in this home. I know that sounds crass and very cold. But you reap what you sow—and she has." Amen to that.

The Laguna Beach police called the tragedy Suicide By Cop.

DEATH IN CALIFORNIA

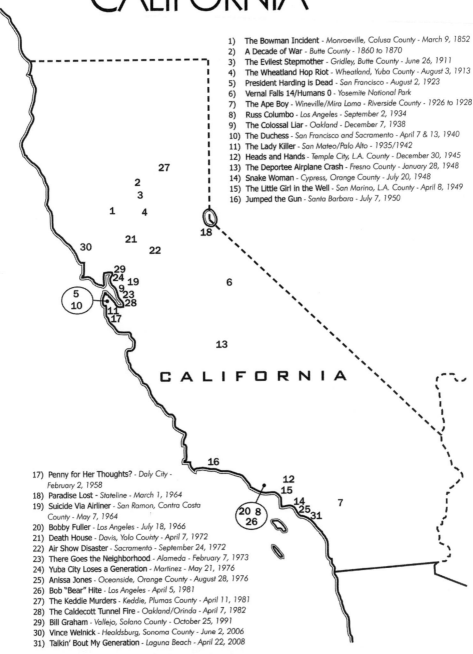

1) The Bowman Incident - *Monroeville, Colusa County - March 9, 1852*
2) A Decade of War - *Butte County - 1860 to 1870*
3) The Evilest Stepmother - *Gridley, Butte County - June 26, 1911*
4) The Wheatland Hop Riot - *Wheatland, Yuba County - August 3, 1913*
5) President Harding is Dead - *San Francisco - August 2, 1923*
6) Vernal Falls 14/Humans 0 - *Yosemite National Park*
7) The Ape Boy - *Wineville/Mira Loma - Riverside County - 1926 to 1928*
8) Russ Columbo - *Los Angeles - September 2, 1934*
9) The Colossal Liar - *Oakland - December 7, 1938*
10) The Duchess - *San Francisco and Sacramento - April 7 & 13, 1940*
11) The Lady Killer - *San Mateo/Palo Alto - 1935/1942*
12) Heads and Hands - *Temple City, L.A. County - December 30, 1945*
13) The Deportee Airplane Crash - *Fresno County - January 28, 1948*
14) Snake Woman - *Cypress, Orange County - July 20, 1948*
15) The Little Girl in the Well - *San Marino, L.A. County - April 8, 1949*
16) Jumped the Gun - *Santa Barbara - July 7, 1950*

17) Penny for Her Thoughts? - *Daly City - February 2, 1958*
18) Paradise Lost - *Stateline - March 1, 1964*
19) Suicide Via Airliner - *San Ramon, Contra Costa County - May 7, 1964*
20) Bobby Fuller - *Los Angeles - July 18, 1966*
21) Death House - *Davis, Yolo County - April 7, 1972*
22) Air Show Disaster - *Sacramento - September 24, 1972*
23) There Goes the Neighborhood - *Alameda - February 7, 1973*
24) Yuba City Loses a Generation - *Martinez - May 21, 1976*
25) Anissa Jones - *Oceanside, Orange County - August 28, 1976*
26) Bob "Bear" Hite - *Los Angeles - April 5, 1981*
27) The Keddie Murders - *Keddie, Plumas County - April 11, 1981*
28) The Caldecott Tunnel Fire - *Oakland/Orinda - April 7, 1982*
29) Bill Graham - *Vallejo, Solano County - October 25, 1991*
30) Vince Welnick - *Healdsburg, Sonoma County - June 2, 2006*
31) Talkin' Bout My Generation - *Laguna Beach - April 22, 2008*

Bibliography

BOOKS

Atherton, Gertrude. *California, An Intimate History*. New York: Blue Ribbon Books, Inc., 1914.

Becker, Chris. *Death in the West: Fatal Stories from America's Last Frontiers*. Flagstaff: Northland Publishing, 2007.

Boyle, Florence Danforth. *Old Days In Butte: A Glamorous Tale of Butte County*. Chico: Association for Northern California Historical Research, 2006.

Brooks, Patricia and Brooks, Jonathan. *Laid To Rest In California: A Guide To the Cemeteries and Grave Sties of the Rich and Famous*. Guilford, Connecticut: The Globe Pequot Press, 2006.

de la Parr, Fito with T.W. and Marlane McGarry. *Living The Blues: Canned Heat's Story of Music, Drugs, Death, Sex and Survival*. Nipomo, CA: Canned Heat Music, 2000.

Drimmer, Frederick. *Until You Are Dead: The Book of Executions in America*. New York: Citadel Press, 1990.

Epting, Chris. *Led Zeppelin Crashed Here: The Rock and Roll Landmarks of North America*. Santa Monica, CA: Santa Monica Press, 2007.

Fein, Art. *The L.A. Musical History Tour: A Guide To the Rock and Roll Landmarks of Los Angeles*. Boston: Faber and Faber, DATE??

Fiorini-Jenner, Gail L. and Hall, Monica Jae. *Western Siskiyou County: Gold and Dreams*. Charleston, SC: Arcadia Publishing. 2002.

Ghiglieri, Michael P. and Charles R. Farabee, Jr. *Off the Wall: Death In Yosemite, Gripping Accounts of All Known Fatal Mishaps in America's First Protected Land of Scenic Wonders*. Flagstaff: Puma Press, 2007.

Guinness Book of Rock Stars: An A To Z of the People Who Made Rock Happen. Edited by Dafydd Rees, Luke Crampton, and Barry Lazell. London: Guinness Books, 1989.

Holland, Barbara. *Hail To The Chiefs: Presidential Mischief, Morals, & Malarkey from George W. To George W.* New York: Berkley Books, 2004.

Hornberger, Francine. *Mistresses of Mayhem: The Book of Women Criminals*. Indianapolis: Alpha Books, 2002.

Mannix, Daniel. *Woman Without Fear: All Creatures Great and Small*. New York: McGraw-Hill, 1963.

McGie, Joseph F. *History of Butte County*, Volume II, 1920 to 1980. Oroville: Butte County Board of Education, 1982.

Nash, Jay Robert. *Bloodletters and Badmen: A Narrative Encyclopedia of American Criminals from the Pilgrims to the Present*. New York: M. Evans and Company, Inc., 1973.

_____. *Murder America: Homicide in the United States from the Revolution to the Present*. New York: Simon and Schuster, 1980.

Newton, Michael. *The Encyclopedia of Conspiracies & Conspiracy Theories*. New York: Checkmark Books, 2006.

Norton, Jack. *Genocide in Northwestern California: When Our Worlds Cried*. San Francisco: The Indian Historian Press, 1979.

Parish, James Robert. *The Hollywood Book of Death*. Contemporary Books. New York: McGraw-Hill, 2002.

Patton, Judge Richard E. *The Bowman Case*. Volcano, California: The California Traveler, 1973.

Perry, Tim and Ed Glinert. *Rock & Roll Traveler USA: The Ultimate Guide to Juke Joints, Street Corners, Whiskey Bars and Hotel Rooms Where Music History Was Made*. New York: Fodor's Travel Publications, 1996.

Pike, Jeff. *The Death of Rock 'n' Roll: Untimely Demises, Morbid Preoccupations and Premature Forecasts of Doom in Pop Music.* Boston: Faber and Faber, 1993.

Pitt, Leonard and Pitt, Dale. *Los Angeles A to Z: An Encyclopedia of the City and County.* LA: University of California Press, 1997.

Rock: The Rough Guide. Edited by Jonathan Buckley and Mark Ellingham. New York: Penguin Books, 1996.

Secrest, William B. *California's Day of the Grizzly: The Exciting, Tragic Story of the Mighty California Grizzly.* Sanger, CA: Word Dancer Press, 2008.

Shenkman, Richard and Reiger, Kurt. *One-Night Stands With American History: Odd, Amusing, and Little-Known Incidents.* New York: Perennial, 2003.

Simmonds, Jeremy. *The Encyclopedia of Dead Rock Stars: Heroin, Handguns, and Ham Sandwiches.* Chicago: Chicago Review Press, 2006.

Stanley, Jerry. *Digger:The Tragic Fate of the California Indians from the Missions to the Gold Rush.* New York: Crown Publishers Inc., 1997.

Strong, Douglas H. *These Happy Grounds: A History of the Lassen Region.* San Diego: Loomis Museum Association, 1973.

Sufakis, Carl. *America's Most Vicious Criminals.* New York: Checkmark Books, 2001.

_____. *The Encyclopedia of American Crime: From Blackbeard to Jeffrey Dahmer.* New York: Smithmark, 1982.

Walker, Dave. *American Rock 'N' Roll Tour.* New York: Thunder's Mouth Press, 1992.

Weaver, John D. *Los Angeles, The Enormous Village 1881–1981.* Santa Barbara: Capra Press, 1980.

Young, Paul. *L.A. Exposed: Strange Myths and Curious Legends in the City of Angels.* New York: Thomas Dunne Books/St. Martin's Griffin, 2002.

NEWSPAPERS

American Weekly
Anaconda Standard (MT)
The Argus (Newark/Fremont)
Billings Gazette (MT)
Cedar Rapids Gazette (IA)
Centralia Weekly Chronicle (WA)
Chicago Daily Tribune
Chronicle-Telegram (Elyria, OH)
Constitution-Tribune (Chillicothe, MO)
Daily Review (Hayward)
Decatur Sunday Review (IL)
East Bay Daily News
Family Weekly
Fresno Bee
Hayward Review
Independent/Press-Telegram (Long Beach)
Jefferson City Post-Tribune (MO)
L.A. Weekly
Life Magazine
Long Beach Independent
Long Beach Press-Telegram
Los Angeles Times
Marysville Daily Forum
Modesto Bee
Modesto News-Herald
Nevada State Journal (Reno)
News and Tribune (Jefferson City, MO)
Oakland Tribune
Orange County Register
Pasadena Star-News
Reptile & Amphibian Magazine
Sacramento Bee
Sacramento Union
San Francisco Examiner
San Mateo Times
Syracuse Post-Standard
Time Magazine

True West Magazine
Valley News (Van Nuys)
Van Wert Daily Bulletin (OH)
Waterloo Evening Courier (IA)

PERIODICALS & JOURNALS

James B. Murphy and David E. Jacques. "Grace Olive Wiley: Zoo Curator with Safety Issues," *Herpetological Review*, 2005, 36(4).

People v. Eggers (1947) 30 Cal.2d 676[185 P.2d 1]

WEBSITES

PoliceOne.com
Franksreelreviews.com
venomousreptiles.org
Check-Six.com
crimelibrary.com

Index

About the Author

Melanie Souza

Born to first-generation Americans in Bay City, Michigan, David Kulczyk (pronounced Coal-check) is a Sacramento-based historian, freelance writer and award-winning author of short fiction. He entered college at the age of 40 after working as a factory worker, sous chef, musician, warehouseman, fish butcher, process server, barista and bike messenger. Kulczyk's work has appeared in the *SF Guardian,* the *East Bay Express,* the *Chico News and Review, Maximum Ink Music Magazine, The Isthmus, Madison Magazine,* the *Seattle Times, Pop Culture Press, Strange Magazine* and the *Sacramento News and Review.* He is also the author of *California Justice: Shootouts, Lynchings and Assassinations in the Golden State* (available from Craven Street Books). Kulczyk lived in Seattle for most of his adult life, with stays in Austin, Texas; Columbus, Ohio; Madison, Wisconsin; and Amsterdam, Uitgeest and Limmen in The Netherlands. He has lived in Sacramento since 2002.